The NAACP
IN WASHINGTON DC

The NAACP
IN WASHINGTON DC

FROM JIM CROW TO HOME RULE

DEREK GRAY

**FOREWORDS BY MARYA MCQUIRTER AND
GEORGE DEREK MUSGROVE**

THE
History
PRESS

Published by The History Press
Charleston, SC
www.historypress.com

First published 2022

Manufactured in the United States

ISBN 9781467140522

Library of Congress Control Number: 2021952404

To all those who have fueled my burning love of history.
And to the individuals in these pages who fought to make a more perfect union by
making their city "mean Democracy's Capital."

CONTENTS

FOREWORD

I have known Derek Gray for more than ten years. We first met in the DC Public Library's Special Collections (now the People's Archive). As an archivist, Derek has been incredibly helpful and generous to me and countless others researching materials at the People's Archive. More recently, I have had the pleasure of working with Derek on several projects commemorating the fiftieth anniversary of 1968. His love and deep knowledge of the archives were invaluable for our collaborations and also shine through in this project.

The NAACP in Washington DC: From Jim Crow to Home Rule is right on time. I'm writing this foreword in September 2021, in the midst of the resurgence of COVID-19 infections and deaths and the afterlife of the white insurrection at the U.S. Capitol in January. While both of these feel brand new, they are also part of a continuum. Washingtonians, individually and organizationally, have been struggling against the lack of full and free health care; the expansion of anti-blackness in and beyond the White House, Congress and the Supreme Court; police terror/ stop and frisk; hyperdevelopment; and taxation without representation. Derek's work offers a much-needed historical context for these struggles through an examination of the D.C. chapter of the NAACP, one of the oldest organizations in the city.

This book is also important because it challenges four well-worn tropes about the history of the city: (1) that there is a singular "Black community" or "Black experience"; (2) that the presence of white liberals is incompatible with white supremacy; (3) that D.C. as a city and a national capital can only be told through the narrative of the supposed contradictions of democracy; and (4) that the use of violence as a strategy was only considered in the 1960s. Derek has provided another model for how to do D.C. history and how to think about the history of the city anew.

While I was reading the book, I kept wondering how some of the more radical members of the NAACP D.C. chapter would think of our current moment and our current organizers and organizations. This wondering does not stem from a desire or need for a narrative of progress but from Derek's insistence on the importance of individual and collective decisions and holding individuals and groups accountable for why and how they make those decisions. I do believe that the more radical members and leaders of the NAACP D.C. chapter would see some of their legacies and desires in the local chapters of Black Lives Matter and Stop Police Terror, which adopt a leaderless approach to organizing and combine multiple strategies, including public rallies, exposing the respectability politics of the mayor and city council and a deep commitment to and grounding in a deep love for us.

The more radical members and leaders of the NAACP D.C. chapter might also see some of the legacies and desires of their campaigns against racism in the Don't Mute DC campaign (which organized in response to white residents attempting to claim U Street as a sonically white space) and the protests against the white-owned Nellie's Sports Bar, also on U Street, which used its "security forces" to claim the business as a white space.

Conversely, Black Lives Matter DC, Stop Police Terror DC and the dozens of other collectives and coalitions may also find the struggles of the D.C. NAACP chapter instructive. Those of us who organize toward freedom and abolition know how challenging it can be—personally, physically, politically, ethically, logistically, financially and intellectually. Perhaps there is solace and renewed energy from a deeper understanding of organizing in the early twentieth century.

Whether you are a Washingtonian, someone researching the history of the city or a history nerd, *The NAACP in Washington, DC* will draw you in. For Washingtonians, Derek draws you in through the institutions he names and maps. You may recognize your church or neighborhood. As a researcher looking for projects, you will find numerous individuals, organizations and events that deserve their own books. And as a history nerd, you will learn more about Nannie Helen Burroughs, W.E.B. Du Bois and Mary Church Terrell, among others. Derek's book offers a treasure trove.

Finally, there have been numerous books on the history of the NAACP. However, *The NAACP in Washington DC: From Jim Crow to Home Rule* is one of just a few books offering a detailed history of a local NAACP chapter. Derek shows us the importance and richness of local histories. I hope others will be inspired to follow suit.

—Marya McQuirter
Anna Julia Cooper Circle/LeDroit Park/D.C.
September 18, 2021

FOREWORD

Washington, D.C., was bound to have one of the most important chapters of the National Association for the Advancement of Colored People. In 1910, the capital city boasted a population of ninety-five thousand African Americans, one of the largest urban concentrations of Black folk in the country. Anchored by Howard University, Freedman's Hospital, the D.C. Colored Schools and the federal government, the community also had a large and politically active Black middle class.

Thus, when D.C. residents established the fourth branch of the association in 1912, it quickly grew to become the largest in the nation. Capitalizing on its size, proximity to Congress and the White House and the pedigree of its supporters—nationally important African American activists and D.C. residents such as Mary Church Terrell, Carter G. Woodson and Nannie Helen Burroughs were early members—it also emerged as one of the most powerful. Under its second president, Archibald Grimké, the branch was a thundering voice of protest against segregation, directly confronting President Woodrow Wilson.

Yet the branch struggled to fulfill its promise.

Granted, the D.C. NAACP was an important player in the local and national struggle for civil rights in its first half century. Towering organizers continued to work through the branch to, as one association publication stated, "Make D.C. Mean Democracy's Capital."

Yet the many important battles of early twentieth-century D.C.—the 1930s "don't buy where you can't work" campaign, the 1940s and '50s struggle to have the District commissioners recognize the "lost laws" and end segregation in public accommodations or the 1960s push for home rule—were conducted in collaboration with the NAACP, not by the D.C. branch itself. Militant branch members like John Davis, Gardner Bishop and Julius Hobson chafed under cautious branch leadership and often did their most important work with other groups or as part of coalitions that allowed them to circumvent the association's more moderate tendencies.

In this wonderful book, Derek Gray helps us to understand this complicated legacy.

As Gray argues, the branch's predominantly elite leadership oscillated "between maintaining acceptance from the white establishment" and "adopting confrontational direct protest tactics." More often than not, when activists and community members demanded militant direct action, "conservatism won out" within the branch.

The NAACP was likely cautious in moments of upheaval because it never succeeded—indeed never tried—to develop a constituency among the Black poor and working class, over 75 percent of the city's Black community for the period under study. Its members, and especially its leadership, were more comfortable in office boardrooms and among the well-heeled. This oversight would sometimes leave the organization a bystander in those critical moments like the late 1930s or 1960s when Black politics shifted toward the needs and aspirations of Black workers and, in turn, away from the NAACP.

But Gray's research also shows the opposite. Though many of them worked with other organizations or left the branch altogether, the D.C. NAACP nonetheless helped to train and equip three generations of African American organizers. And it supplied crucial legal backing and elite contacts for some of the very direct-action protesters who criticized its timidity.

The story herein, then, is one of a critical though imperfect organization. It is as much inspiration as cautionary tale. And we are fortunate that it has now been told.

—George Derek Musgrove
Assistant Professor of History
University of Maryland–Baltimore County

ACKNOWLEDGEMENTS

*T*his book may not have come to fruition had it not been for the many people who walked through the doors of the Washingtoniana Division (now the People's Archive) in the Martin Luther King Jr. Memorial Library between 2008 and 2015 seeking information about civil rights activism in Washington, D.C.

By the summer of 2015, my interest in the District of Columbia branch of the NAACP had been sparked by these inquiring minds. When did the branch form? Why? What were its victories? Its challenges? Its defeats? Who were the players? Now, thanks to these patrons, I know the answers. More importantly, I am grateful for the opportunity to share them.

A number of people are responsible for the completion of this project. A huge thank-you to the retired Jeff Flannery and the Manuscript Division staff at the Library of Congress. Each of my numerous trips there from 2018 to February 2020 to research the NAACP records was enjoyable, productive and rewarding. Many thanks to former curator Joellen El Bashir and former photo librarian Meaghan Alston at Howard University's Moorland-Spingarn Research Center for pointing me in helpful directions beyond my original research requests and for the generous support with image reproductions. A special thank-you to Judy Williams, Shiloh Baptist Church historian, for all her assistance when I was hunting for photographs of Reverend John Milton Waldron, the first president of the D.C. branch of the NAACP.

Thanks to former research services librarian Jessica Smith (DC History Center), Jessica Eichlin (West Virginia and Regional History Center),

Michael Hosking (Harpers Ferry National Historical Park), Vanessa Broussard and Alison Oswald (Smithsonian National Museum of American History), Kimberly Springle (Charles Sumner School Museum and Archives) and Kerrie Williams (former manager of The People's Archive at the DC Public Library).

Some of the history of the D.C. NAACP is connected to Richmond, Virginia, where I previously lived and worked. So it makes sense that my research path stretched south to the Library of Virginia, my old stomping ground. A big shout-out to my colleague and friend reference archivist Cara Griggs for assisting me with some Confederate organization mysteries.

Thanks to Sarah Shoenfeld, historian/principal of Prologue DC, for providing thoughtful and brutally honest feedback on the manuscript. I cannot emphasize how much I appreciated her valuable insight. I am greatly indebted as well to Dr. Marya McQuirter and Dr. George Derek Musgrove, two griots of Black DC history, for their moving forewords to this book.

Special thanks to The History Press for the opportunity to publish, and most certainly to my editor, Kate Jenkins, whom I have truly enjoyed working with over the past four years. Writing during a pandemic has been both comforting and stressful. Aside from her obvious editorial skills and expertise, Kate's support, guidance, humor and patience (sorry for all those missed deadlines!) has made this experience a most fulfilling one.

Finally, I am grateful to my mother, Corryn Gray, for supporting me throughout this journey.

Thanks to you, the reader, for picking up a copy of this book. Enjoy!

INTRODUCTION

The cardboard church fans that the eight hundred mourners inside Lincoln Congregational Temple at 1701 Eleventh Street NW in the heart of the historic Black Shaw neighborhood were waving for any kind of relief from the sticky, one-hundred-degree heat were not doing much good. They had waited a long time. Doors opened at 10:30 that July 29, 1954 morning—almost three hours before the homegoing for ninety-year-old civil rights activist Mary Church Terrell began. It took a while for the procession of thirty-four cars, taking up an entire city block reserved by five African American and white police officers, to arrive. But no one was impatient. Finally, an organ prelude opened the service, followed by an invocation from Reverend C. Shelby Rocks, a rendition of "O Love That Will Not Let Me Go," several Scripture readings and Rocks's reading of the obituary. It lasted no more than forty-five minutes. It could have been longer, but there was not much else to say. Everything went "the way she would have wanted it," the Baltimore edition of the *Washington Afro American* reported. "Mary Church Terrell passes into history as one of the truly great women of her time," wrote the *Washington Evening Star*, the city's white daily newspaper. "Mrs. Terrell had preached her own funeral through her many years of service to humanity," the Black-owned *Atlanta Daily World* wrote in tribute.[1]

Terrell was affiliated with numerous civil rights organizations throughout her life, but many of those years of service were with the District of Columbia branch of the National Association for the Advancement of

Colored People. She was a founding member of both the national organization in 1909 and its Washington branch in 1912. Terrell's memorial service was the obvious focus that day, but the branch's presence was visible. Maxwell Rabb, President Dwight Eisenhower's associate White House counsel, came to pay his respects of his own volition. George E.C. Hayes, one of Terrell's pallbearers, could have offered a terse greeting or ignored him completely. An attorney, Hayes had been a member of the branch since 1918, chaired its legal committee and was elected its president on a mild autumn evening in November 1944 at the church. He served until April 1947, tackling recreational segregation. In the early 1950s, he was a key figure in *Bolling v. Sharpe* and *District of Columbia v. John R. Thompson Co., Inc.*, two U.S. Supreme Court cases that

Mary Church Terrell, founding member of the national NAACP in 1909 and its District branch in 1912. *Library of Congress (LC-DIG-ppmsca-37806).*

challenged segregation in the city's schools and restaurants, respectively. The latter case was initiated and won by Terrell, but the president eclipsed her success, an action to which she took umbrage: "I was as provoked as I could be when I read in the newspapers this morning that the Eisenhower Administration was taking credit for this victory." And on this day, no official White House representative was present for her funeral. Eisenhower declined an invitation to attend, claiming he did not know Terrell personally. Nevertheless, Hayes was gracious. He invited Rabb to sit with him and the other pallbearers.[2]

Lincoln was a landmark of civil rights activism in the capital and much of the branch's history was rooted in the congregation. In 1913, its members, determined to make their organization work for Black Washingtonians and prevent it from being used as a tool of political patronage, ousted disgraced president John Milton Waldron, pastor of Shiloh Baptist Church, in a raucous meeting there. In 1916, the branch met at Lincoln to plot a strategy to prevent the screening of D.W. Griffith's racist film *The Birth of a Nation*. Robert Brooks, the longtime Lincoln minister and chair of the branch's education committee, eulogized Archibald Grimké, its second president, in 1930 at the church. In 1940, after a two-year dispute with the national office that almost led to its demise, the branch allied with other organizations at Lincoln to form the Washington Civil Rights Committee. In 1963, the church, coordinating with the branch, opened its doors "to about one thousand" attendees of the March on Washington for Jobs and Freedom "for a hearty breakfast at nine" and "freedom songs." In 1966, the thirty-year-old future "Mayor for Life" Marion Barry, as leader of the District's Student Nonviolent Coordinating Committee (SNCC) and its "Free DC" Movement, led a discussion at the branch's Lincoln meeting on the topic "Black Power: Good or Bad?" Arguing that integration still "had not reached the masses" in Washington, Barry encouraged parents to advocate for the teaching of African American history in schools. "The Negro should not be ashamed of his blackness but should organize around it."[3]

EARLY CIVIL RIGHTS ACTIVISM IN D.C.

African Americans in Washington had branded their home as the "Jim Crow Capital" by the 1930s to express how societal conditions mirrored those living in the South. In a city that memorialized presidents who proclaimed the United States a democracy, the presence of Jim Crow was a chilling contradiction. But it had not always been that way. Andrew Johnson's presidency ushered in a period of resistance to Black advancement and empowerment, but by the late 1860s and early 1870s, the racial climate had shifted dramatically and reflected the hope of a true democracy emerging from a devastating civil war. As the nation moved toward Reconstruction, Congress passed the District of Columbia Voting Rights Act of 1867, granting Black men the right to enfranchisement, three years before the Fifteenth Amendment was enshrined in the Constitution.[4]

In 1869, Black men integrated the city's police and fire departments, were appointed as ward commissioners and held the position of public health physician. Ulysses S. Grant, the new Republican president, signed laws permitting Black men to serve on juries. The charters governing the City of Washington and Georgetown no longer applied to just "white" citizens, as that distinction was removed. In 1872 and 1873, under laws passed by the territorial legislature, restaurants, parlors, hotels and other private businesses prohibited discrimination. Violators of these decrees were "fined one hundred dollars" and compelled to "forfeit his or her license as keeper or owner." The *Star* acknowledged that the changes were "quite a revolution." However, it was a short-lived one. By 1878, Washington was ruled by a three-member board of commissioners, and residents lost control of local governance. Although this transformation did not include a repeal of the anti-discrimination statutes, they were not enforced either. These "Lost Laws" became the foundation of the civil rights movement in the city during the 1950s.[5]

In May 1896, the Supreme Court's infamous 7–1 *Plessy v. Ferguson* decision cemented "separate but equal" as the law of the land, favoring the Louisiana edict for separate Black and white passenger railroad cars as a reasonable exercise of state power. Referred to as the "Jim Crow car case" by newspapers, the decision was the culmination of several previous rulings that had slowly eroded African Americans' rights since the 1857 *Dred Scott* case. The court had provided an official seal of approval on the myth of white supremacy and endorsed a racial caste system. For Justice John Harlan, the lone dissenter, *Plessy* had further ingrained that myth in the American psyche. "There is no caste here," Harlan wrote in his opinion. "In respect of civil rights, all citizens are equal before the law."[6]

The branch's founding followed in a long line of civil rights activism in Washington. African American women were pioneers in its earlier movements. The dismal *Plessy* decision rallied the Black community, particularly the many "colored women's clubs" that had organized in 1895 to protest segregation and lynching, improve child welfare and extol the virtues of Black womanhood. Two nationally representative bodies of African American women—the Colored Women's League (CWL), formed in the District by Terrell and fellow activist/educator Anna Julia Cooper, and the National Federation of Afro-American Women (NFAAW) in Boston—gathered in Washington two months after *Plessy* for their conventions. Although the ruling could not be reversed, it is likely that the city was selected to ensure their collective voices of protest would still be heard by the president, Congress and the Supreme Court. The CWL held its convention first, July 14–16 at the Fifteenth Street Presbyterian Church; the NFAAW followed suit at the Nineteenth Street Baptist Church (NSBC) from July 20 to 22. Dr. Walter Henderson Brooks, the NSBC pastor, gave a warm welcome. Their presence, he said, was "a happy indication of the dawning of a brighter and better day, when the best women of the land unite…to lift up and ennoble the womanhood of the race."[7]

Several of the most influential Black women in the nation joined Terrell at the conventions, including journalist and anti-lynching activist Ida B. Wells-Barnett; Tuskegee Institute "Lady Principal" (and wife of Tuskegee founder Booker T. Washington) Margaret Murray Washington; and Josephine St. Pierre Ruffin, a journalist, suffragist and editor of the *Woman's Era*, the first

Right: Activist and educator Anna Julia Cooper, co-founder of the Colored Women's League in the District, was a member of the NAACP's D.C. branch and its drama committee. *Library of Congress (LC-DIG-bellcm-15413).*

Below: The Nineteenth Street Baptist Church, located on Sixteenth Street NW, was a prominent venue for civil rights activism in the late nineteenth century. The National Federation of Afro-American Women of Boston held its convention there after the *Plessy v. Ferguson* Supreme Court decision in May 1896. *DC Public Library.*

IDA B. WELLS.

Left: Journalist and anti-lynching crusader Ida B. Wells-Barnett was one of many Black women activists to join Mary Church Terrell at the Colored Women's League's convention at the Nineteenth Street Baptist Church in Washington in July 1896. *Library of Congress (LC-USZ62-107756)*.

Below: Members of the National Association of Colored Women at Harpers Ferry in 1896. They are in front of the engine house where John Brown was captured after his 1859 attack on the federal arsenal. *Harpers Ferry National Historical Park*.

national newspaper published by and for African American women. To the glorious delight of the delegates, abolitionist and heroine Harriet Tubman, then eighty years old, also attended. Upon their conventions' conclusions, the groups merged to become the National Association of Colored Women (NACW). Terrell was elected as its first president for a term that would expire in 1901. The NACW adopted the motto "Lifting As We Climb," a soaring message to demonstrate to "an ignorant suspicious world that our aims and interests are identical with those of all good, aspiring women." It became the largest and most influential civil rights organization in the country. In the capital city, the NACW advocated for suffrage rights, quality education for Black students and the abolition of the convict release system. Several of its official objectives strongly paralleled the future national NAACP and its District branch:

> *To secure and use our influence for the enforcement of civil and political rights for all citizens.*
>
> *To promote interracial understanding so that justice and good will prevail amongst all people.*[8]

The Niagara Movement and the Formation of the NAACP

In 1905, the debate between W.E.B. Du Bois and Booker T. Washington concerning viable solutions to Black advancement culminated in the founding of the Niagara Movement in Ontario, Canada. By the end of the year, the movement boasted 170 members with chapters in twenty-one states and the District of Columbia. Its second meeting took place in Harpers Ferry, West Virginia, from August 15 to 18, 1906, at the historically Black Storer College in honor of John Brown's raid on the federal arsenal. The conference had the workings of both a business convention and spiritual revival. Meetings and discussions were held on securing civil rights, followed by a march from the college to the Murphy Family Farm (the site of the historic fort where the incident reached its bloody climax), where, in a ceremony of remembrance, the participants removed their shoes and socks to honor the sacred ground on which they stood.[9]

Many studies on the Niagara Movement often ignore the participation of African American women and their roles in the activities of the Washington

Above, left: Historian, author and Niagara Movement founder W.E.B. Du Bois supported the branch's work by publishing much of its activities in *The Crisis*, the NAACP's magazine, and speaking at its meetings when he visited Washington. *Library of Congress (LC-DIG-ppmsca-38818).*

Above, right: Tuskegee Institute founder Booker T. Washington advocated economic prosperity over racial equality in his 1895 "Atlanta Compromise." *Library of Congress (LC-USZ62-47451).*

Opposite: W.E.B. Du Bois and other founding members of the Niagara Movement superimposed over an image of Niagara Falls, Canada. *Library of Congress (LC-DIG-ppmsca-38818).*

chapter of this early civil rights organization. Several female members of the D.C. chapter also later organized the District's NAACP branch, including Carrie W. Clifford, Martha Waldron and Charlotte Forten Grimké (sister-in-law of Archibald Grimké, the second branch president). They coordinated general membership meetings at the Nineteenth Street Baptist Church and were prolific fundraisers. Even before Clifford settled with her family in Washington in 1910, she secured financial contributions from parishioners at Shiloh Baptist Church and Plymouth Congregational Church in 1908 and 1909, respectively. Hailing these women, Du Bois later described the Harpers Ferry gathering as "one of the greatest meetings that American Negroes ever held."[10]

Deadly race riots in Atlanta, Georgia (1906), and Springfield, Illinois (1908), led to the founding of the NAACP in New York in 1909. Although there

was no violence in Washington that year, the city was still entrenched in racist southern culture. In October 1906, Terrell powerfully contradicted the claim that the District was the "colored man's paradise" that many professed it to be in a speech at the United Woman's Club. In her address, "What It Means to Be Colored in the Capital of United States," she

Niagara Movement women at Harpers Ferry. Some members of its D.C. chapter, like Charlotte Hershaw (*standing, far right*), organized the D.C. branch of the NAACP. *Library of Congress (LC-DIG-ppmsca-37818).*

said, "For fifteen years, I have resided in Washington, and…it has been doing its level best ever since to make conditions for us intolerable. Surely nowhere in the world do oppression and persecution based solely on the color of the skin appear more hateful and hideous than in the capital of the United States."[11]

With the birth of the NAACP, the notion that Black and white could not join together to fight for racial justice and equality in education, housing, transportation, public policy and more was debunked. It was now a reality. However, the association's New York City headquarters limited its power and guaranteed a test of strength in the battles that came. Although it was the largest city in the country, New York was not Washington, where ideas were introduced, debated and passed into law and where issues of national interest took form in the halls of Congress. This new organization would need a presence in the District of Columbia.

This book chronicles the work of the Washington, D.C. branch of the NAACP from 1912 to 1973. The narrative traces its early formidable crusade against President Woodrow Wilson's segregation policies and analyzes its dual role as both a watchdog body to prevent the passage of legislation in Congress that negatively affected African Americans nationally and as the leading organization advocating on behalf of the interests of the city's Black community. It examines the association's victories and defeats against numerous Jim Crow campaigns and practices in employment, law enforcement, education and local affairs as well as its relationship to the competing civil rights organizations in the District from the New Negro Alliance in the 1930s to the Congress of Racial Equality, Southern Christian Leadership Conference, Student Nonviolent Coordinating Committee and the Black United Front in the 1950s and 1960s.

Throughout this period, the branch, founded by the city's African American elite, resisted efforts to represent the interests of all Black Washingtonians regardless of class. Its leaders oscillated between maintaining acceptance from the white establishment through conservative accommodation and adopting confrontational direct protest tactics to advance and empower Washington's Black communities. Ultimately, conservatism won out.

Despite these challenges, this book is a story about how a prominent civil rights organization conveyed a simple, but important, message through its work: "Make D.C. Mean Democracy's Capital."

1

"A LIVELY RESPONSE WAS MANIFESTED"

*I*t was inevitable that an NAACP branch would be established in Washington, D.C. In 1910, the city numbered ninety-five thousand Black residents, comprising almost 30 percent of the total population. The M Street High School and Howard University served as powerhouses of quality Black education, and prominent African American attorneys, educators and entrepreneurs boasted a thriving upper-middle and elite class.[12]

Local "vigilance committees," later called "branches," sprouted across the country when the NAACP was created. John Milton Waldron was perfect to lead one in the District. A Washington Vigilance Committee formed in 1910, and Waldron quickly assumed control of it, working diligently to support the organization with speeches and public rallies. Heralded in the press as "a leader in many good movements," Waldron served as the first president of the city's branch of the NAACP when it formally organized on March 20, 1912.[13]

John Milton Waldron was born in Lynchburg, Virginia, on May 19, 1863, to parents of Black, Native American and Scotch-Irish descent. Educated "in a little log cabin schoolhouse" in neighboring Amherst County, he took preparatory training courses at the Richmond Institute (now Virginia Union University) and received a bachelor's degree from Lincoln University in Pennsylvania in 1886. A desire to enter the ministry led him to the Newton Theological Institute, a predominately white divinity school in Newton Center, Massachusetts, where he finished his studies in 1889. Waldron

John Milton Waldron served as the first president of the branch when it formally organized in March 1912. He was ousted in August 1913 after a stormy leadership tenure. *Shiloh Baptist Church Archives.*

John Milton Waldron served as pastor of Shiloh Baptist Church, located in the historic Shaw neighborhood, from 1907 to 1929. *DC Public Library, Star Collection © Washington Post.*

briefly returned to Virginia in 1890 and worked as a missionary with the Young Men's Christian Association in Richmond. He rose to prominence quickly as general secretary with the organization and served as a pastor and editor of various religious journals.[14]

Between 1890 and 1907, Waldron developed a ministry style that earned him a reputation as one of the country's most progressive theologians. His divinity education in Massachusetts introduced him to the concept of the "institutional church," a central element of the Social Gospel movement of the late nineteenth and early twentieth centuries. This philosophy considered an individual's social and economic well-being to be equally as important as their spiritual needs.[15]

After two years at Berean Baptist Church in Washington and fifteen at Bethel Baptist Church in Jacksonville, Florida, Waldron returned to the District to lead Shiloh Baptist Church in 1907. He had broadened his appeal as a pastor and proponent of racial self-help and established a record of fighting for racial justice by leading protests against Jacksonville's segregation ordinances. Waldron also came to the capital as the treasurer of the Niagara Movement, which enabled him to wield great influence as the organization's chief financial officer. He served as treasurer until February 1909.[16]

Waldron and the
Alley Improvement Association

Waldron's ministerial work with the city's poorest Black residents helped cement his election as branch president. Poor health and unsanitary housing conditions that bred disease and crime plagued the District's working class as early as the 1870s. The death rate among African Americans from tuberculosis alone was 283.3 per 100,000 residents. As Black people comprised the majority of occupants of dilapidated structures tucked into alleys within distance of more immaculate houses, it was a concern to the Black community. During this period, the board of health began to condemn these places, but the 1879 Organic Act halted its power and authority.[17]

Efforts to reform alley dwellings gained traction at the dawn of the twentieth century. A 1904 investigative report on housing conditions led Congress to create the Board for Condemnation of Insanitary Buildings in 1906. In 1907, President Theodore Roosevelt established the President Homes Commission, a fifteen-member body to assess alley life and recommend improvements. Its findings led Black religious, education and temperance

Many of the most impoverished living conditions in Washington during the early twentieth century were in its alleys. These conditions led to the establishment of the Alley Improvement Association in 1908. Waldron served as its first president. *DC Public Library.*

John Milton Waldron (*second from right*), as president of the Alley Improvement Association, tours the slums of Navy Place SE with several members of Congress and District commissioners. *Library of Congress (LC-DIG-npcc-01553).*

leaders to form the Alley Improvement Association (AIA) in September 1908. Waldron served as one of its directors and soon became its president. The pastor brought various organizations—including the Association for the Preservation of Tuberculosis, Women's Interdenominational Missionary Union, Colored YWCA, and the Day Nursery Association—often to Shiloh to "appeal for workers and money" to help "2,000 white and 17,000 Negro alley dwellers."[18]

By 1910, the AIA had visited all 266 alleys in the city and secured low-rent housing for Black dwellers with support from the Sanitary Improvement Company, razing several alleys in the process. The reforms were successful; the alley population declined from nineteen thousand in 1906 to eleven thousand in 1915. The association also tended to the spiritual well-being of these residents with religious open-air meetings, prayer services and Sunday schools in their spaces. As the AIA's workers were mostly Shiloh parishioners, Waldron welcomed alley children at the church each year for the summer vacation Bible school.[19]

FORMATION OF THE WASHINGTON, D.C. BRANCH OF THE NAACP

In early March 1912, a group of elite Black men and women organized to establish an NAACP branch in the District. There were just three temporary officers and no constitution or executive committee members. Lafayette Hershaw, a veteran of the Niagara Movement, was selected to be president. Carrie Clifford served as vice president. William Henry Richards, an attorney and Howard University professor and law librarian, was designated treasurer.[20]

It was time to acquaint the public with the branch's work on behalf of equality, liberty and justice and to expand membership. A large venue was vital once a sign-up list of interested people reached two hundred, and a ten-person "committee of arrangements" that included Hershaw, Mary Church Terrell and Waldron was created to ensure a successful meeting. On March 19, the group selected Metropolitan AME Church both for its size and the opportunity to host the gathering in conjunction with a meeting of the Bethel Literary and Historical Association (BLHA), which the church hosted regularly.[21]

The joint event was sensible, as the branch and the BLHA fit each other perfectly as forums for racial issues in the District. Founded at Union

The D.C. branch of the NAACP was organized at Metropolitan AME Church in March 1912. *DC Public Library, Star Collection © Washington Post.*

Bethel AME Church (the predecessor of Metropolitan) in 1881 by Bishop Daniel A. Payne to encourage an educated ministry and congregation, the BLHA attracted an audience larger than church members by 1883. Most of Washington's Black elite were members of the prestigious organization. Racial issues, the progress and well-being of African Americans nationally and a prideful emphasis on African heritage were popular subjects at meetings and lectures. Many Black Washingtonians who formed the District NAACP were also members of the association, including Terrell,

Archibald Grimké, historian and scholar Carter Godwin Woodson and Kelly Miller.[22]

The national office yearned to spread its message in Washington, and the guest speaker list reflected this enthusiasm. Du Bois was invited to address the meeting, as was Joel E. Spingarn, president of the New York City branch and professor of comparative literature at Columbia University, who later served the NAACP as treasurer, president and chairman from 1913 until his death in 1939. James Morton, an attorney, and Martha Gruening, Oswald Garrison Villard's secretary at the *New York Evening Post*, rounded out the roster. A prominent local individual would preside over the meeting. That honor went to Wendell Phillips Stafford, associate justice of the D.C. Supreme Court. The arrangements committee also decided that the meeting would conclude with joyous entertainment. A request was made to and accepted by the Howard University Glee Club to perform for the evening.[23]

Although Du Bois canceled his appearance due to illness, the other speakers presented on the new organization's work and goals with specific details, general calls for action and philosophical rhetoric. Spingarn aroused interest by informing his audience about the discrimination battles engaged by the New York City branch, with a focus on the state's new civil rights law. Morton followed suit, enveloping Spingarn's presentation into a general appeal for human rights and the importance of the NAACP's mission to counteract against "agencies devoted to the spread of race prejudice." Gruening promoted *The Crisis* and reported on the association's tireless work against lynching. Deciding not to close her remarks on a morbid note, she regaled the audience about the artistic talents of Richard Brown, a young rising painter.[24]

Waldron closed the meeting with a request to Washingtonians to advocate for the NAACP and join the branch. *The Crisis* reported that "a lively response was manifested." Indeed, it was. Attendees took up an impressive collection of ninety-eight dollars, many subscribed to the magazine and seventy-five became members. Others wrote messages indicating their desire to take an active role in the new branch and voted to schedule a future date to establish a permanent organization.[25]

That date turned out to be the very next day, in which a full slate of new officers was elected. Waldron became the branch's president. Hershaw was elected chairman of its five-member executive board. Mary Church Terrell replaced Carrie Clifford as vice president. Clifford joined the executive committee. Benjamin Griffith Brawley, a Howard University English professor, was elected to the new position of secretary. George William Cook,

Left: Between 1913 and 1939, Joel Spingarn served as board chairman, treasurer and president of the NAACP. He was one of the speakers at Metropolitan AME Church when the D.C. branch organized. *Library of Congress (LC-DIG-ppmsca-05524).*

Right: Wendell Phillips Stafford, associate justice of the D.C. Supreme Court, was one of the D.C. branch's few white members. *Library of Congress (LC-DIG-hec-21069).*

a Howard alumnus who also held the positions of instructor, dean and alumni secretary, replaced William Henry Richards as the new treasurer. A constitution was also adopted and sent to the national NAACP headquarters for approval. The two-day meetings were so productive that Spingarn, overjoyed with enthusiasm, extended his Washington visit by adding speaking engagements at Howard and the M Street High School. Membership had increased to 143 persons. Success had been achieved. The D.C. branch, joining the other three in New York, Boston and Chicago, was born.[26]

Waldron's stellar civil rights background, pastoral leadership and position as branch president did not translate into immediate support and robust membership numbers for several reasons. Although the national NAACP believed that a Washington branch was necessary to monitor and report on congressional activity relevant to its interests, its executives did not take an assertive role to assist Waldron in expanding membership. As a Niagara Movement member, Waldron was in New York City with Du Bois to form the NAACP in 1909. Although its initiatives and resolutions passed successfully,

Waldron and civil rights activist William Monroe Trotter took issue with nearly every one and expressed their views sharply in opposition. Their behavior irritated colleagues, many of whom believed that both men had degraded themselves with petty griping and wasted valuable time to conduct important business. Tensions may have lingered from the dissension.[27]

A second factor that impeded immediate support for the association for many years was the optics of its very own body. To its founders, the biracial harmony reflective in the formation of the NAACP was a strength that would draw support and expand membership to conquer the nation's racial woes. Public meetings composed of both Black and white members were held, but the leadership also identified other strategies to encourage cross-racial contact and dialogue. African Americans were invited to speak on white college campuses, and invitations were extended to white speakers to address audiences at historically Black colleges and universities. Interracial parlor gatherings were also held to maintain the appearance of a united front.[28]

However, support was minimal, as few white people actually participated in these events. One sobering example that underscored the severity of this problem was a 1911 meeting in New York that addressed lynching. Villard,

Charles Edward Russell, journalist and co-founder of the NAACP, was one of the D.C. branch's few white members. Russell chaired its Interracial Committee in the 1930s. *Library of Congress (LC-DIG-ppmsca-23825).*

who organized the group, was disappointed when prominent white individuals he singled out to attend did not, nor did they speak out to raise public sentiment against the terror of vigilante mobs.[29]

As Du Bois was director of research and publications and editor of *The Crisis*, his position was prestigious and crucial to the organization. However, he was the lone African American officer on the executive committee. By contrast, William Walling (chairman), Moorfield Storey (president), John Milholland (treasurer) and Villard (co-founder and second treasurer) were all white men. If Black advancement was its founding principle, why did this new organization not have more African American representation?

A third factor was a lack of connection to the District's African American population. There was a sharp contrast between the organization's white leadership and the

Black D.C. branch. Charles Edward Russell and Stafford were just two of its few white members. Neither man was a native Washingtonian. Russell was a "muckraker" journalist from Iowa who came to Washington after several unsuccessful campaigns for political office in New York. A recess appointment to the D.C. Supreme Court by President Theodore Roosevelt brought Stafford to the capital from Vermont in 1904. Whether due to a lack of interest in the livelihood of Black residents or a lack of awareness that a community of people of color wished to tackle the city's racial troubles, white Washingtonians did not align themselves with the D.C. branch and its causes.[30]

Resistance from the White and Black Press

As the driving force of public opinion, the white and African American press played a significant role in the tepid embrace of the NAACP in its infancy. This was the greatest obstacle for the branch. The *Washington Post* and *Star* served as the two major daily newspapers covering the District and neighboring Virginia and Maryland. The *Post* did not report about the branch's initial public mass meeting at Metropolitan AME Church. It also did not promote the call for membership several days before as the *Afro American* had done with its March 16 edition. Even with Waldron's selection as president, he was featured only in articles about the Alley Improvement Association between March and May.[31]

Although the *Star* reported on the NAACP meeting, its coverage was still mediocre. The Metropolitan event was published on April 13, twenty-five days after the gathering. The *Washington Times*, another white newspaper, also reported the meeting that day. Just like the *Post*, the *Star* also made no effort to raise awareness about the organization before March 19 as the *Afro* had done. In addition to the three-week delay, details in the *Star* announcement were disappointingly scant. The newly elected officers and executive committee members were identified, but no information about proceedings (such as nominations, candidate statements) or other related business was provided. Biographical information about the guest speakers (Spingarn and Gruening) was excluded. Excerpts of speeches and summations of presentations also went unreported.[32]

The *Star* resorted to unusual practices of reporting on the branch when it organized. Articles were merely terse announcements that relayed the meeting date, time and venue and little else. At times, a guest speaker was identified, but post-meeting coverage was scarce. Even the placement of meeting notices was bizarre, if not disrespectful. Whether the content was obscurely located at the bottom of a page deep inside the newspaper or sandwiched between other eye-catching headlines, it was easy for readers to overlook branch news. In one example, a brief December 1912 article about a public meeting the next day at Zion Baptist Church was jammed between a longer one about a jailed young African American woman's suicide attempt before her trial sentencing and an advertisement for hemorrhoid ointment that was guaranteed to cure in "6 to 14 days."[33]

The branch fared no better with the African American press. A broad-shouldered, towering man at six-foot-three, William Calvin Chase wielded much influence and power with the city's Black elite as the publisher and editor of the *Washington Bee*, which operated from 1882 to 1922. Under his leadership, the *Bee* focused on thoughtful, critical articles condemning racial discrimination and prejudice and called on the federal government to protect citizens and identify ways to ameliorate people's lives. Its masthead was "Sting for Our Enemies—Honey for Our Friends." Members of D.C.'s African American community who worked tirelessly to advance equality and inspire youth were deemed "race men and women" who deserved the latter part of the bold motto. Those who did not bore the wrath of the former.[34]

Chase had a firebrand perspective on racial pride. He scorned political movements and societal organizations established to uplift African Americans that also included even the most liberal white members. This was the primary factor in his opposition to the NAACP. Chase provided no coverage to Villard's "Call" that initiated the association's founding and dismissed the new organization for more than one year. However, by November 1910, he could no longer ignore its existence nor Du Bois's prominence. Chase's rebuke of both was one of the most vivid examples of the *Bee*'s promise of "Sting for Our Enemies." In a harsh critique, Chase commented on other past short-lived organizations that focused on securing Black civil rights and accused the NAACP of being yet another new "movement." He struck at Du Bois indirectly, focusing on the Niagara Movement, of which the Atlanta professor was the chief architect: "What has become of the Niagara Movement, which was brought into the world a few short months ago to reform everybody and everything? What has become of the Equality League, the Constitutional League, and all the rest?"[35]

It may have been lost on Black Washingtonians, but Chase's words exemplified a clever, but misleading way to manipulate public opinion in the District. The Equality and Constitutional Leagues were indeed founded and wholly supported by white men, but they dissolved mostly due to dissension from personality differences and jockeyed maneuvering for organizational control. It was not because the membership was biracial. However, to Chase, the new NAACP would be more of the same—a movement that would never thrive and fail quickly. After all, he reasoned, Du Bois worked in an organization that was run by white men. His office was located in a building owned by a white man. The executive committee members were in control of Du Bois. He could talk only when they wanted him to talk, write only what they wanted him to write and "go and come" only when they wanted him to do so.[36]

The bitterness Chase leveled against Du Bois and the association also had much to do with the competition of yet another business rival. Four other African American newspapers (the *Grit*, *Leader*, *Colored American* and *Argus*) operated in Washington when Chase began publishing the *Bee* in 1882. In 1908, he ran into financial difficulties when another Black newspaper, the *Washington American*, appeared. *The Crisis*'s first issue in November 1910 laid out its mission to function as the NAACP's publication. Financed by white backers and produced in the capital by the Murray Brothers Printing Company (owner Freeman H.M. Murray was a Du Bois ally), its production posed another economic threat to Chase. His anxiety was justifiable; its circulation dramatically increased from one thousand to twenty-four thousand copies in its first six months, with most going to the Black elite in New York, Chicago and Washington. Chase's criticism of Du Bois also conveyed a peculiar irony: a man who had garnered a reputation for fiery condemnation of racism and established a career rooted in that passion also appealed to it by portraying Du Bois as a white man's lackey.[37]

Although Chase eventually became a member of the branch and the *Bee* became more supportive of the NAACP's advocacy efforts in the city, early opposition to the organization came at a time when its infancy status mandated immediate support. News by and about the association was available in *The Crisis*, but it was offered only as a benefit of membership. Thus, Chase provided a disservice to Black Washingtonians by depriving them of knowledge of the branch and its agenda.

Outspoken and headstrong, Waldron would later become entangled in several self-inflicted leadership crises, resulting in his expulsion. A new president would take over, mobilize the membership and lead the organization into battle against an unexpected and powerful foe: the new president of the United States. But that path would be long and treacherous for the young branch.

2

THE RISE AND FALL
OF THE "PREACHER-POLITICIAN"

I was born and raised in the South. There is no place easier
to cement friendship between the two races. [38]
—Governor Woodrow Wilson addressing the United Negro
Democracy of New Jersey, 1912

He intends to treat every man with justice and fairness if he is elected President. [39]
—John M. Waldron on Wilson's candidacy, 1912

Tuesday, March 4, 1913, was Inauguration Day. It was a chilly fifty-five degrees. Shortly after one o'clock in the afternoon, Thomas Woodrow Wilson, the former governor of New Jersey, placed his hand on an open Bible and was administered the oath of office as the twenty-eighth president of the United States by U.S. Supreme Court chief justice Edward Douglass White, a Confederate veteran. Thin and bespectacled, Wilson stood "at the center of [a] vast, humanity-filled amphitheater at the east front of the Capitol" looking more like the historian and Ivy League university president that he once was. His physical stature and demeanor were in stark contrast to the portly, mustached and jolly-faced William Howard Taft who had taken his oath four years before inside the Capitol during a raging blizzard and who would soon happily depart with his family for Georgia. Although the crowd erupted into reverberating cheers, the overcast sky and the "simplicity and lack of pomp" of the ceremony, as the *Star* reported, fit well with the new president's stoic personality. [40]

Left: President Woodrow Wilson galvanized the D.C. branch to protest his administration's segregation polices in the federal workforce. *Library of Congress (LC-USZ62-5139).*

Below: President Wilson at his first inauguration on March 4, 1913. *Library of Congress (LC-USZ62-51391).*

Born on December 28, 1856, in Staunton, Virginia, Wilson was the first southerner to enter the White House since Andrew Johnson, and the first Democrat since Grover Cleveland before the turn of the twentieth century. Wilson attended Davidson College in North Carolina for the 1873–74 school year but transferred to the College of New Jersey (now Princeton University), where he studied political science and history. Armed with a doctorate in political science from Johns Hopkins University in 1886, he lectured at Bryn Mawr College and Wesleyan University before finally settling down at Princeton as a professor of politics and jurisprudence after rejecting calls to join the faculties of Johns Hopkins and the University of Virginia.[41]

Wilson rose steadily through the ranks at Princeton, first as chair of jurisprudence and political economy, then its president. He championed and implemented many reforms, including the institution of academic departments and a system of core requirements. He embraced religious diversity as well with faculty appointments of the first Jew and Catholic, but that inclusion extended only so far. For his entire tenure as its chief executive, Wilson utilized his power to prevent African Americans from enrolling at Princeton at a time when the Ivy League was beginning to open its doors to small numbers of Black students.[42]

THE 1912 PRESIDENTIAL CAMPAIGN

Wilson's ascendancy to the White House in 1912 began four years before. Democratic Party leaders knew of his interest to be on the 1908 ticket, but it was not meant to be that time. However, in 1910, New Jersey Democratic powerbrokers, impressed with Wilson's Princeton leadership, laid the groundwork to make him their candidate in that year's gubernatorial election. Wilson won easily, defeating his Republican opponent, Vivian M. Lewis, by a margin of more than 650,000 votes. He was inaugurated on January 17, 1911, as the Garden State's thirty-fourth governor.[43]

Wilson's tenure was marked with the passage of antitrust legislation in a state that was notoriously dubbed the "Mother of Trusts" because it shielded corporations from other states' antitrust laws. His timing was perfect. The presidential election of 1912 was approaching, and the Democrats needed someone who could recapture the White House after years of Republican control. Nominated in Baltimore, the governor faced three other opponents in a remarkable four-way race that included Taft, who was seeking reelection, and Theodore Roosevelt, the former president who had ascended to the White House after William McKinley's assassination and was seemingly done with politics after his departure in 1909. Rounding out the group, Eugene Victor Debs, an Indiana trade unionist and founding member of the Industrial Workers of the World, was the nominee of the Socialist Party of America.[44]

The four men offered Americans bold economic reforms. However, race was the elephant in the room that none of them addressed, and it was a marginal topic in the election. The Democratic and Republican conventions did not place the subject in their party platforms, and no candidate prioritized it in a stump speech or policy debate. Each man had a troubling record on racial equality. Taft deferred to white southerners in making federal appointments, and in a speech cloaked in racial paternalism, he noted approvingly that "the Negro…is coming more and more under the guardianship of the South." The president also refused to take executive action against lynching or even issue public condemnations. And there were many—more than three hundred during Taft's entire term.[45]

Although Roosevelt had appointed several Black men to government positions and invited Booker T. Washington to dine at the White House in 1901, the former president also took no valiant effort against lynching. As the new Progressive Party's nominee, he capitulated to white southerners, who comprised the convention organizers, to exclude Black delegates, a move that contradicted the new party's name. African Americans were particularly stung by Roosevelt in August 1906. In Brownsville, Texas, 167 members of the all-Black Twenty-Fifth Infantry Regiment were discharged without honor after false charges were made and incriminating evidence was planted that 12 of the men had embarked on a shooting rampage that killed a white bartender and wounded a white police officer. The soldiers were ineligible to receive their pensions and permanently barred from seeking federal civil service jobs.[46]

A dramatic exodus of African American voters from the Republican Party to the Socialists to ensure a win for Debs was an inconceivable notion, but even still, the third-party candidate made no effort to include or speak to Black voters. Instead, he was prone to make "darky" jokes in public, a societal norm in 1912 America. Wilson did not rise above this insensitive behavior either, regardless of geography. Such jokes were made on the campaign trail in the South, as well as with northern audiences. During a speech about the unpopular Payne-Aldrich Tariff Act, Wilson went for a chuckle by referring to a foreign item in it as a "nigger in the woodpile."[47]

It was not just these words that raised eyebrows about Wilson. Although some Democratic operatives predicted that Black support would ensure a victory for the governor, some Black observers cautioned that definitely remained to be seen. The *New York Age*, an African American newspaper that tilted Republican ideologically, was more than skeptical, questioning in a scathing editorial how any self-respecting Black man or woman could bring themselves to cast a vote for Wilson. Its charges were credible: Wilson did not appoint any African Americans to his cabinet as governor. The party

Oswald Garrison Villard, grandson of abolitionist William Lloyd Garrison, was a founding member of the NAACP. A friend and early supporter of Woodrow Wilson in 1912, he worked with the D.C. branch against Wilson's segregation of the federal workforce. *Library of Congress (LC-DIG-ppmsca-37818).*

platform at the Democratic convention in Baltimore did not contain a single word about Black people, an action that Wilson could have prevented. Under his leadership, Princeton was the only major university that kept its doors closed to African Americans. The *Age* also opined that Wilson owed his nomination to two ardent white supremacist senators: James K. Vardaman of Mississippi and South Carolina's Benjamin Tillman. "Both by inheritance and absorption, he [Wilson] has most of the prejudices of the narrowest type of Southern white people against the Negro," it said.[48]

Having now morphed from academician to politician, Wilson said all the right things that resonated with African American voters. Lynchings had torn at the social fabric of the nation since the birth of the Ku Klux Klan in 1866 and increased dramatically during the Reconstruction era, even before Tuskegee Institute began keeping official records in 1881. So when Oswald Garrison Villard, a Wilson friend and supporter, reported that the governor told him emphatically that he would condemn extralegal killings as "every honest man must do," African Americans took him at his word. And many were just as impressed and pleased when he said it. The promise had not come in the middle of a heated race that would have looked like a pivot from one issue to another. And had Wilson made such a bold declaration at the close of the campaign, it would have been considered a last-minute, desperate appeal to the Black voter. Instead, it came at the beginning.[49]

Wilson also began his campaign with a message of hope for interracial unity and brotherhood in the one place in the nation that seemed the most unlikely: the South. A Virginian by birth, he reasoned that he could speak frankly on the subject. Addressing a delegation of the United Negro Democracy of New Jersey, he stated, "I was born and raised in the South. There is no place easier to cement friendship between the two races." He also spoke with Villard at length about the establishment of a National

Commission on Race, which, although met with enthusiasm, was vague on details, goals and purpose. In the final days before Election Day, Wilson wrote an open letter to AME bishop and NAACP vice president Alexander Walters in which he assured the civil rights leader that Black Americans could expect justice from his presidency on all matters and "executed with liberality and cordial good feeling." He also added, "They may count upon me for absolute fair dealing…in advancing the interests of their race in the United States." By this point, Wilson had captivated African Americans, and many believed that he sincerely had their aspirations at heart.[50]

DU BOIS ENDORSES WILSON

Du Bois had a clear preference among the candidates even as he emphasized that African Americans faced "desperate alternatives" in November. *The Crisis* provided an ideal platform to reach Black voters. Taking advantage of the opportunity to exert influence in a presidential campaign, he endorsed Wilson in its August issue. Laced with odd contradictions, the statement

African American newspapers accused Woodrow Wilson of owing his 1912 presidential nomination to politicians like Mississippi senator James Vardaman (*holding hat*), who once said, "If it is necessary, every Negro in the state will be lynched; it will be done to maintain white supremacy." *Library of Congress* (*LC-DIG-ggbain-13322*).

was pillared on a tepid embrace of the man personally, the power of the Black vote and a direct challenge to the Democrats to pursue and harness it. Wilson, Du Bois argued, had never been a friend to African Americans and would not be in the White House either. He had demonstrated that with his racially exclusive policies at Princeton. But then he pivoted, describing Wilson to readers as "a cultivated scholar," assuring them "he has brains" and exonerating him from his Virginian heritage and Princeton decisions: "A man, however, is not wholly responsible for his birthplace or his college." It was a bizarre defense. While the birthplace reference was true, as Princeton's president, Wilson was indeed completely responsible for keeping African Americans out of the school. And for a Black man who was among the firsts in Ivy League academia successes (the first to earn a doctorate from Harvard University) and also a professor himself, Du Bois should not have considered Wilson's actions a moot issue.[51]

Nevertheless, Du Bois believed that Wilson gave African Americans hope because he did not possess the beliefs or speak the ugly racism of the more vocal purveyors of white supremacy within the Democratic Party like Tillman and Vardaman. Nor would he sign any legislation sponsored by these men that would further disenfranchise African Americans. "He will not advance the cause of the oligarchy of the South…and he will remember that the Negro in the United States has a right to be heard and considered." Above all else, Du Bois believed that the Democrats' economic message would benefit Black America most.[52]

WALDRON AND WILSON

As cautiously optimistic as Du Bois and Villard (who represented the national NAACP) were about Wilson, Waldron was more enthusiastic. He endorsed Wilson in his gubernatorial bid through his National Negro American Political League (NNAPL) in late October 1910. "We feel that you are worthy of the loyal support of every liberty-loving, fair-minded citizen—especially every manly, independent colored voter," he wrote, while also offering Wilson organizers, speakers, canvassers and any other services that he desired.[53]

Waldron and several prominent African American pastors from Washington, Cincinnati and New York who had fought alongside him during the Niagara Movement formed the NNAPL in June 1908. Its purpose was to ensure the Republican Party remained loyal and supportive to Black interests. Smaller, defunct civil rights groups like the Constitution League and Afro-American Council also comprised the new organization. Waldron's stellar civil rights and ministerial career had its benefits; he was elected its president unanimously.[54]

The 1908 presidential election was an opportunity to test the NNAPL's power and influence, but it failed. Waldron met with party officials "to demand fair play for the Negro" but was dismissed. Seeking revenge, the NNAPL did not support the Taft-Sherman ticket. Members voted to endorse the Democrats at its meeting on August 10 at the True Reformer Building at Twelfth and U Streets NW, named for the Black fraternal Grand United Order of True Reformers and also designed, constructed and financed by African Americans. Much to Waldron's chagrin, Taft won the election, but it was not a complete disappointment, as the NNAPL cut into his coattails, successfully defeating Republican candidates for Congress in Illinois, Indiana, Massachusetts, New Jersey, New York and Ohio. It was a valuable lesson for Waldron, as he concluded that Black interests and advancement should be supported by individuals and their ideas, not political parties. The organization soon became the National Independent Political League (NIPL) to reflect race neutrality and added powerful mottos to reflect a commitment to suffrage, liberty and unity for all citizens: "In a Republic the Ballot is the Citizen's Most Powerful Weapon" and "A United People Is a Powerful People."[55]

Waldron remained a thorn in Taft's side for much of his term, challenging him on his lack of action on racial matters and criticizing him for his sense of prejudice against African Americans. By 1912, the NIPL had decided to make him a one-term president. On July 11, nine days after the Democratic National Convention in Baltimore, Waldron sat down in his home at 1334 V Street NW and wrote to Wilson, indicating the NIPL's interest in his campaign. He proposed a meeting with its representatives, and Wilson accepted. Although they never formed a warm friendship, correspondence indicates the two men had a cordial and professional relationship. Waldron soon became Wilson's most ardent supporter among the civil rights community in Washington as the city's NAACP president. He spoke glowingly of the governor in speeches and interviews, but it was during this time that Waldron's troubles in leading the branch slowly began to formulate.[56]

In late August, Waldron traveled to Portsmouth, Virginia, to preach the gospel at the Lott Carey Baptist Foreign Convention. He managed to provide a wide-ranging interview to the *Virginian Pilot-Norfolk Landmark* covering equal rights, independent voting, the power of the ballot for the Black man, the NIPL's role in five Democratic gubernatorial victories and, of course, Woodrow Wilson. The governor had met with delegations from various African American organizations by this point, but his joint meeting with Waldron and William Monroe Trotter (whose *Boston Guardian* newspaper served as an official arm of the NIPL) garnered more attention. Dismissing Taft and Roosevelt curtly for the same reasons Du Bois laid out in *The Crisis*, Waldron heaped praise on Wilson. "His manly, straightforward bearing…his practical insight into the great issues which confront this country…his transparent honesty, as well as his assertion that he intends to treat every man with justice and fairness if he is elected President—all greatly impressed our representatives," he boasted. African Americans had nothing to fear, Waldron said, because Wilson's "sense of chivalry and loyalty…which have always characterized the old-time Virginia gentlemen" would enable him to get the "so-called race problem settled." Wilson was the ideal candidate.[57]

Waldron's statements were amusing. It remained to be seen how a "gentleman" who had kept Princeton's doors closed to Black students would work to solve the "so-called race problem." However, another part of the interview was more bewildering. Waldron characterized the relationship between Black people and white southerners as "our best friends in everything essential except politics." In all aspects of life, they were strong allies. Southern white men built African American churches, would conduct business with black businessmen "as no other men will," had taken care of Black elders, employed African Americans "by the millions" and "readily" lent money to Black borrowers. The most ludicrous of his litany was his view on interracial relations in defense and protection. White southerners, he stated, "defend us when in trouble and sympathize with us in distress."[58]

Waldron's fictional depiction of race relations overshadowed everything else in the interview. Civil rights leaders yearned for the day when his words would become a reality, but at that moment, they were a fantasy, particularly when he addressed sympathy and defense. As Black men and women often died at the hands of white lynch mobs, the criminal justice system in the South was anything but just. And these killings drew hundreds (sometimes thousands) of spectators who took human body parts as "souvenirs" and posed for photographs next to mutilated or charred corpses that appeared in newspapers or were distributed as postcards, to the glee of bystanders. So how did white southerners defend and sympathize with African Americans in trouble? And as a veteran of the Niagara Movement, civil rights warrior in Florida, founder of the NAACP and now president of its branch in the capital, what had Waldron been fighting for all this time if the racial landscape in the South was so picturesque? Did Waldron even believe what he was saying, or was it an effort to capitulate to Wilson's philosophy? Was he expecting something in return for this support?

Back in Washington, if the branch membership was disillusioned with their president's message in Portsmouth, they did not reveal it. At this point, Waldron was a well-respected leader in the city and a mover and shaker in the apparatus of national politics. He led a loyal congregation at Shiloh. His Alley Improvement Association was credited by the Black elite and middle classes with the betterment of predominately African American residents living in squalid conditions. And in October 1911, shortly after Waldron took the helm at Shiloh, his theologian peers elected him president of the Interdenominational Ministers' Association, a prominent African American organization. Waldron had become a celebrity.[59]

He got his wish on Election Day. After a bitter campaign, the electorate turned to Wilson, the political novice. He won forty states for an impressive landslide victory total of 435 electoral votes. Republicans' split between Taft and Roosevelt gave the governor the opening he needed. Roosevelt won California, Michigan, Minnesota, Pennsylvania, South Dakota and Washington, totaling 88 electoral votes. Only Utah and Vermont remained loyal to the president, giving Taft a dismal 8. Voters were not at all enamored of socialism or its messenger, and they let Debs know it: he carried no states and garnered not a single electoral vote. Waldron believed he now had an ally at 1600 Pennsylvania Avenue. He would soon learn how wrong he was.[60]

FEDERAL SEGREGATION IN THE WILSON ADMINISTRATION

In early spring 1913, several weeks after the inauguration, John Skelton Williams, the new assistant treasury secretary and a native of Powhatan, Virginia, was unprepared for and appalled at what he encountered one evening when he visited the Bureau of Engraving and Printing: white and African American women "working together and opposite side each other." He went to Joseph Ralph, the bureau's director, and informed him that the new administration would no longer permit such workplace practices and requested something be done about it.[61]

Ralph and other agency officials were not immediately supportive of segregating their employees, as they regarded such a policy as "impracticable." However, they complied. Separate lunch tables for Black workers were set up in the rear of the bureau cafeteria. Even toilets and lockers became segregated. The changes did not offend or discourage white employees. In fact, they were emboldened by them. Some complained about their African American colleagues. Rose Miller, a white employee in the Wetting Division, filed a formal grievance about her Black supervisor, Louise Nutt. Ralph replaced her within a week.[62]

Segregation in Washington's workplaces was not a new phenomenon. It had existed since Theodore Roosevelt's presidency. In 1904, the Bureau of Engraving and Printing had a "Jim Crow corner." After the controversial Washington-Roosevelt meal, it would be a long time before another Black person was ushered into the White House for a similar event. Nothing changed when Taft came into office; the dining room had a racial line of demarcation for employees as well. Only several agencies in the federal government allowed Black workers, and they worked separately from their white colleagues in what was quietly referred to as "Negro colonies." Even Mary Church Terrell's husband, Robert, the trailblazing first Black municipal judge in the country, was subjected to such indignities. Several years before Taft blessed him with a successful nomination, Terrell worked in the Treasury Department. Lunchroom workers there refused him service.[63]

What was new was an aggressive wave of anti-Black sentiment shared by a group of men at the highest levels of government who had the power and determination to transform their philosophies into policy. The new president was a southerner who packed his cabinet with like-minded men who never recanted their Confederate biases. For them, a gut-wrenching reality existed in the nation's capital that had seemed unimaginable fifty years after Gettysburg: Black men and women bossing white men and women.[64]

It all began one day at one of Wilson's first cabinet meetings. The agenda was to implement new policy. Albert Burleson, the new postmaster general, had an idea. He wished to segregate not only all the African American and white employees in the Postal Service but also those in all departments. Burleson had enormous influence with the new president. Wilson was a newcomer to Washington politics, but the eight-term congressman from Texas definitely was not. The son of a Confederate officer, Burleson was well known for his segregationist views, but in 1913, that was no disqualifier or liability. He knew the inner workings of Congress, had a great relationship with House

Postmaster General Albert Burleson proposed segregating African American and white employees in the Postal Service at one of President Wilson's first cabinet meetings. *Library of Congress (LC-USZ62-62930)*.

majority leader Oscar Underwood and was an ally of Speaker Champ Clark, the two men Wilson would definitely need to make his "New Freedom" a reality.[65]

For African Americans, however, Burleson was the worst possible choice for postmaster general; the Post Office was the largest employer in the country and one of two federal agencies in Washington with a high number of Black employees. He would be the boss of more African Americans than any other individual. The railway mail service employed a significant number of men of color. An integrated workforce would eventually lead to an alarming increase of racial resentment and friction since, according to Burleson, white men had a better work ethic and always outperformed their Black colleagues. He struck a sympathetic tone when he noted that these men could and should not deal with the difficult labor while sharing water fountains and sinks with their darker-hued co-workers: "It is very unpleasant for them to work in a car with negroes where it is almost impossible to have different drinking vessels and different towels, or places to wash."[66]

The other agency was the Treasury Department, and here another segregationist was its administrator. Wilson installed William McAdoo as the new secretary. A native of Georgia and Tennessee, McAdoo and the president knew each other before Wilson's gubernatorial days. McAdoo prospered in business affairs and built a successful career as a railroad entrepreneur. A man of the Progressive Era with an emphasis on growth over profits, advocacy of equal pay for women and the "The public is pleased" motto that he lived by professionally, he fit neatly into the new administration. Toeing the line of the eventual official policy requiring the separation of the races in Washington's federal departments, his views were clear: "I shall not be a party to the enforced and unwelcome juxtaposition of white and negro employees when it is unnecessary and unavoidable without injustice to anybody, and when such enforcement would serve only to engender race animosities detrimental to the welfare of both races and injurious to public service."[67]

Unfortunately, that was all just one side of it. When Wilson woke up the morning after the election, he did not inquire about the details of his historic victory first. Instead, he wanted the congressional results, hoping he received what every new chief executive wants: coattails. He had them. The Sixty-Third Congress (March 4, 1913–March 4, 1915) began with Democrats solidly in charge; the party had gained sixty-one seats in the House and strengthened its Senate majority by seven. Wilson told reporters that the results gave him "the hope that the thoughtful Progressive forces of the Nation may now at last unite to give the country…a Government…devoted to justice and progress."[68]

William McAdoo, secretary of the treasury, also segregated African American and white employees in the Treasury Department. *Library of Congress (LC-USZ62-33041).*

That statement rang hollow for African Americans, particularly those in the District. The new Congress was one of the most racially hostile in the history of the legislative body. Its opening was not until April 7, but Representative Frank Clark of Florida wasted no time on that first day, introducing two bills to segregate streetcars and prohibit interracial marriage in Washington. Identical resolutions had been introduced by southern Democrats on both subjects as early as 1906 but never passed due to Republican control of the chamber. Born in Alabama and raised in Georgia as the son of a Confederate veteran, Clark brought forward three similar measures even before Wilson's election and would sponsor eight more through 1920. Representative James Aswell of Louisiana introduced a bill to segregate the races in the national civil service, the first of its kind. It was just one of two proposals Clark sponsored for the entire session; he argued it would be "fair to both races and pleasing to the right-thinking Negro." Not to be outflanked, Representative Charles Edwards of Georgia wrote a bill that called for all Black and white employees in the entire U.S. government to be segregated.[69]

Waldron's Troubles Begin

While the grousing about integrated workplaces boiled in the White House and on Capitol Hill, Waldron triggered his downward spiral in the former capital of the Confederacy. At a meeting of the Dunbar Literary and Historical Society at Richmond's Third Street African Methodist Episcopal Church in late March 1913, Waldron spoke of the need of friendship between African Americans and white southerners. The tenets of his speech were a refrain of the *Virginia Pilot-Norfolk Landmark* interview, but Waldron struck a more caustic tone this time. If the Black man wanted to remain a citizen, he declared, he had no choice but to "renounce the bugaboo of allegiance to the Republican Party" and learn to vote for the best candidate if he wanted to retain that right.[70]

The speech resulted in a wave of criticism from branch members. Waldron could have made a powerful case on the importance of the right to vote regardless of candidate or political party and left it at that. But he condescended African Americans' loyalty to the Republican Party and suggested that Black disenfranchisement was due to this affiliation. The party had been founded to abolish slavery, and emancipation had come under a Republican president. Waldron's implication that African Americans were slaves to the party and had to be taught the right way to vote was arrogant and insulting. Many believed that he had crossed a line.[71]

It did not end there. When the branch formed, members hoped to begin a scientific study of the District's Black schools to improve them, as they suffered from an unequal allocation of funding from the city. A friend would be needed in that endeavor, and Roscoe Conkling Bruce, the assistant superintendent of the "colored" schools, qualified as a potential advocate. But Waldron attacked the devoted Bruce as an ineffective leader, a move rooted in Waldron's dislike of Booker T. Washington, of whom Bruce was an ally. However, the move backfired due to Bruce's pedigree. Mississippi senator Blanche Kelso Bruce and women's rights activist and socialite Josephine Beall Wilson Bruce, both popular and well-respected among the Black Washington elite, were his parents.[72]

Waldron continued to self-destruct. He wrote to Black government employees requesting one-dollar payments to maintain the Washington headquarters of the NIPL. Those who did, according to the *Bee*'s reporting, would "be protected in all ways." Letters and official correspondence poured in from the South, but Waldron retained them instead of forwarding them to the national office. He took it upon himself to issue proclamations and

Joseph Patrick Tumulty, President Wilson's personal secretary, notified the NAACP that John Milton Waldron requested the president consider him for recorder of deeds. The move triggered Waldron's ouster as branch president. *Library of Congress (LC-USZ62-99298).*

resolutions on national and international affairs. Waldron traveled to New York for NAACP business on several occasions and inappropriately used branch funds to cover all his expenses. Regarding the branch as the most powerful in the country, he issued a threat to the national headquarters that he could eventually dominate the organization from the capital. Then, when Black federal workers began suffering the indignity of segregated government offices and appealed to the branch for assistance, Waldron offered none.[73]

Miraculously, Waldron was reelected president at the branch's meeting at Shiloh on the evening of April 18. The agenda was packed: the constitution had to be amended, other officers had to be elected and several delegates were to be selected for the upcoming national NAACP convention in Philadelphia. It appeared that Waldron would survive his troubles, but one action finally doomed him. He wrote to Joseph Patrick Tumulty, Wilson's private secretary, and requested that the president appoint him recorder of deeds, a prestigious post that Black men, including Frederick Douglass, held exclusively in the capital for the past thirty-two years.[74]

It was impossible for Waldron to deny his intent. Tumulty sent the letter to Villard along with a twelve-page memorandum from Robert Hudspeth, a white New Jersey Democratic official, listing the names of prominent Black men who deserved to be rewarded for their support of Wilson. Waldron was on the list. It was now clear that the pastor was illegally using the branch presidency to obtain a highbrow political appointment.[75]

WALDRON'S OUSTER AS BRANCH PRESIDENT

Members were livid and fed up with Waldron at this point. Several prominent individuals initiated a grassroots campaign to remove him as president. They included Lafayette Hershaw; Carrie Clifford; Nannie Helen Burroughs, president of the National Training School for Women and Girls; and Neval H. Thomas, a history teacher at Dunbar High School. The national executive board joined forces with the local branch, but the lily-white body saw the controversy more as an opportunity to rein in the power of the all-Black branch. On May 6, the board had a meeting in New York and discussed the organization's affairs in Washington. On May 17, NAACP founder Mary White Ovington drafted an instructional memorandum for May Childs Nerney, a white woman in her mid-thirties who joined the NAACP in 1912 as its secretary after a career as a reference librarian in Newark, New Jersey. The D.C. branch controversy was raised, and "it was decided that the secretary [Nerney], then absent, should be directed to take up two points with the Washington members."[76]

The first was "the advisability of having an advisory committee composed of prominent colored and white men, the majority white men." Suggested individuals would come from all walks of life: "a number of men in the House and Senate, Grand Army men, etc." The board wanted to also consider Howard University "men who had been prominent in the Negro cause for a decade," an apparent reference to the Niagara Movement. Although faculty members like Benjamin Brawley and George William Cook were officers, they were not, according to the Board, civil rights veterans like Hershaw, who had been with the movement from its inception.[77]

The second point was about Waldron himself. Expressing gratitude for "Dr. Waldron's fearless position for many years," the board concluded his posturing as a Democratic partisan "would unduly antagonize many Washington people whose help we need." Ovington also confirmed that they knew he was "an applicant for office," referring to Waldron's letter to the White House, which "Mr. Villard received and sent us to file." The memo omitted the other issues, but the board decided to take its case directly

NAACP co-founder Mary White Ovington proposed an advisory committee "composed of prominent colored and white men, the majority white men" as a response to John Milton Waldron's troubles in leading the branch in May 1913. *Library of Congress (LC-DIG-ppmsca-23826).*

to Waldron. The leaders were assured that "he would understand our point."[78]

He did not. With Nerney present, the board members discussed the matter with Waldron, but he rejected their conclusion that he was a hindrance to the NAACP's work in the District. Several members of the branch's executive committee also attended, armed with a "memoranda" from Nerney recommending Waldron's removal either by voluntary resignation or a vote of the committee or the general membership. The committee chose the latter when Hershaw made a motion for Waldron to resign. The branch president retorted that he "did not intend to take the advice of Mr. Villard or the advice of the Executive Committee" and would leave only if he was "crucified by his own people at a branch meeting." Hershaw's motion was not seconded by the committee, and no action was taken.[79]

On June 16, the committee tried unsuccessfully to remove Waldron a second time. Four days later, he was crucified by his own people at Lincoln Congregational Church. His attempts to clear the floor of members who presented charges against him almost spurred violence at the raucous meeting. Those present cursed at Waldron "in a most vile manner"; bedlam engulfed the meeting as ominous shouts of physical harm reverberated throughout the room: "Take him out the chair!" "Mob the president!" Throw him out the window!"[80]

Angered that their church "was being desecrated" and fearful that everyone risked arrest for disorderly conduct, officers ordered Waldron "to cease the meeting at once." He complied, adjourning the gathering after a second motion. At 11:00 p.m., three hours later, many members still remained inside Lincoln. They went to another part of the church, held a factional meeting and voted to appoint Hershaw chairman of the proceedings. His first motion was to declare the office of the president vacant. Carrie Clifford, who had been elected vice president in April, was designated interim president on top of her vice presidential duties. Waldron

Above: John Milton Waldron was ousted as branch president during a meeting at Lincoln Temple Church in June 1913. *Lincoln Temple Church Archives.*

Opposite: Neval Thomas (*second row, far right*) taught history at Dunbar High School and was one of John Milton Waldron's detractors. He served as the branch's second president from 1925 until his death in 1930. *Moorland-Spingarn Research Center, Howard University.*

was now a leader with no following. On June 27, the faction drafted a new thirteen-point constitution and forwarded it to the board for approval with Clifford and Acting Secretary Thomas Clarke's signatures.[81]

It was not approved, and the branch remained in turmoil for the summer of 1913 as Waldron's fate was decided. The national office was his last line of defense when board members decided to address the matter at their July 1 meeting. In an angry letter on June 28, Waldron demanded an impartial hearing and urged them to consider his deep ties to the organization and its founding principles of justice and fairness. "As a loyal member of the leading Branches and one of the founders of the national Body and of the DC Branch, I demand full and exact justice…and I shall not be content with anything less," he concluded.[82]

Waldron's supporters weighed in with messages to New York dismissing the factional group. His enemies demanded his removal. Freeman H.M. Murray, the Washington correspondent of the *Boston Guardian* and a diehard ally, preferred to address the only Black man on the board and wrote Du Bois from his home at 1733 Seventh Street NW "to state a few facts and a few opinions regarding the situation." Either the board had been misinformed, Murray wrote, or it was deliberately "just playing cheap, out-

DUNBAR FACULTY

Top to bottom, left to right:

Mr. William D. Nixon	Mr. Charles L. Pinderhughes	Mr. Louis H. Russell
Dr. Georgianna R. Simpson	Miss Clarissa M. Scott	Mr. Neval H. Thomas
Mr. Daniel B. Thompson	Miss Ruth E. Weatherless	Mrs. Alice M. Williams
Miss Etta L. Williamson	Mr. James C. Wright	Mr. John H. Williams

15

of-date politics." Most of the members were actually "old and dependable militants" like Waldron and himself. Murray concluded that the pastor simply dared to represent "the hateful radical Democrat which our people have been schooled to fear and distrust." He urged Du Bois to relay to the board that the rebels' actions at Lincoln that night were "clearly illegal."[83]

Thomas was appointed the factional group's spokesperson. He appealed to Joel Spingarn, who was now the NAACP's first chairman, cautioning Waldron's future with the branch would be problematic even if he was permitted to retain the office. "The loyal people in the cause at Washington will not follow Dr. Waldron," he wrote. The opposition to the minister also had as much to do with what he represented as it did with his illegal and unethical activities. Waldron epitomized the Black "preacher-politician" that people like Thomas, Burroughs and Clifford despised. The domination of minister leadership was evident in every facet of the city's African American community. This was especially the case with the schools, to which Thomas and Burroughs (both teachers), took particular umbrage. This traditional social structure was excoriated by Waldron's detractors, who believed this old order had produced selfish, manipulative leaders who sacrificed the gains African Americans had made for their own pursuit of ascension to power and influence. It was time for new leadership.[84]

Waldron did not prevail. The board took no action at its July meeting but removed him from office in August. His troubles had cost the organization dearly, as the board dealt the branch a harsh blow by also punishing the membership. "We find that the National Association for the Advancement of Colored People has no official branch in the District of Columbia," Spingarn concluded as chair of the Committee on Branches. Signed by Spingarn, Nerney and attorney Charles Studin, the committee proposed two recommendations to ameliorate the crisis: (1) only members who had dues paid "up to and including June 20th" would be recognized as constituting a new, official branch and (2) a new constitution would be created that would include a requirement for an election of officers in which the candidates would be selected only by the Committee on Branches.[85]

Clifford wrote to the board that these actions were excessive and unnecessary. She complained that Waldron should have been expelled immediately and the entire conflict had drawn precious time away from important civil rights work. Although he removed himself from politics by resigning from the NIPL and withdrawing his name for the recorder of deeds appointment, his troubles, she lamented, had resulted in the branch's loss of a year's worth of activism.[86]

As interim president, Clifford was frustrated. There was much work to do, and with Wilson elevating a racial crisis, the NAACP could not afford the absence of a branch in the capital. What would be the outcome?

3
NEW BATTLES AND A "RED SUMMER"

*A*rchibald Henry Grimké observed the rancor in Washington from his home in Boston with disgust. He was with Waldron as one of the organizers of the branch in March 1912 but later informed the national office that he would never fully participate in its activities as long as it was being led by "self-servers like Dr. Waldron." The officers in New York took Grimké seriously, and with good reason. His family was one of several—the Terrells, Cooks and Wormleys—that had provided Black activist leadership in the District for many generations. Grimké's brother, Francis, was a member of the Niagara Movement, founder of the NAACP and pastor of the city's Fifteenth Street Presbyterian Church, which had a large African American congregation and was an important center of Black elite life in the city. His wife, Charlotte Forten Grimké, the granddaughter of the famous abolitionist James Forten of Philadelphia, devoted much of her life to educating the formerly enslaved. Archibald's daughter, Angelina, who would engage in the branch's fight to prevent the showing of *Birth of a Nation* in Washington in 1916, was named for her white great-aunt Angelina Grimké, wife of the late abolitionist Theodore Weld. She once described her father as "a consistent and uncompromising fighter, all his life, for the welfare of his race."[87]

Born into slavery near Charleston, South Carolina, on August 17, 1849, Grimké attended freedmen's schools and graduated from Lincoln University and Harvard Law School. He settled in Massachusetts shortly afterward and spent much of his life and career in Boston. In August 1883, Grimké became editor of the *Hub*, a Republican newspaper that served the city's Black community. He supported gender equality and suffrage rights as he connected the movements for African Americans and women as part of the same struggle. At just thirty-four years old, Grimké already was among the nation's most highly regarded Black leaders, including William Monroe Trotter (co-founder of the *Boston Guardian*), T. Thomas Fortune (editor and publisher of the *New York Age*), William Calvin Chase (editor of the *Washington Bee*) and Booker T. Washington.[88]

Journalist, attorney and diplomat Archibald Grimké was appointed interim president of the branch in September 1913. Formally elected in January 1914, he served until January 1925. *Moorland-Spingarn Research Center, Howard University.*

Grimké switched political parties in 1888 and campaigned for Democratic president Grover Cleveland's reelection. It was a blessing for him. In 1894, he was rewarded with an appointment as consul to Santo Domingo in the Dominican Republic. He had joined an exclusive group of honorable Black diplomats, including Frederick Douglass, who had served in Haiti. In October 1895, he traveled to Washington to receive his official confirmation and stayed with his brother at his residence. He arrived in the Dominican Republic—a nation settled and dominated by people of African descent—on November 16, 1895.[89]

Grimké proved to be an adept negotiator in his ambassadorial role and exhibited leadership skills that would later encourage the national office to recruit him to resolve the crisis in the fledgling D.C. NAACP. The country's president, General Ulises Heureaux, was a challenge. Ruthless and cold, he had risen politically due to his military experience and wanted full independence from America while still seeking its investments to improve the nation economically. However, the two men became close friends and met often, with Grimké serving as an intermediary with foreign investors; they both shared the same goal of eliminating the Dominican Republic's horrid poverty. More importantly, Grimké believed his experience demonstrated that there was hope for America on the racial front. The United States

Francis Grimké, pastor of the Fifteenth Street Presbyterian Church and a member of the Niagara Movement, was Archibald Grimké's younger brother. *Moorland-Spingarn Research Center, Howard University.*

was a multiracial place and so were the nations of the Caribbean with their African, Indian and Spanish peoples. There was no racial animosity, Grimké observed, and the Dominican Republic could serve as a model to how Black and white citizens back home could live and prosper together peacefully. His primary concern was not the political stability that America could bring to the nation but "colorphobia" and prejudice if Heureaux's republic became influenced by America. "There will appear for the first time there [*sic*] also cruel caste distinction, race contempt and insolence and plenty of them, race rule, inequality, and oppression and no end of them, such as curse today the colored people of the United States."[90]

In 1897, President McKinley rejected the extension of Grimké's appointment to Santo Domingo. He returned home and immersed himself in Black politics with divided time in Washington at Francis and Charlotte's home and in Boston at an acquaintance's boardinghouse. He allied with Du Bois against the "Tuskegee Machine," joined the Niagara Movement and later the NAACP. In 1903, he served as the president of the American Negro Academy (ANA), an elite group of intellectuals that sought Black upliftment through nonconfrontational methods. Membership excluded the poor, the working class and women and was limited to just fifty individuals, although it never reached that number. Grimké's affiliation with the prestigious organization disappointed some Washingtonians given his support for equality for women in Boston. Initially established as the African Institute by William Crogman and Alexander Crummell in 1894, the ANA struggled to sustain support as its members became involved in other organizations like the branch and advocated protest action over the publication of academic analyses as a means to combat racism and discrimination.[91]

GRIMKÉ TAKES CONTROL OF THE BRANCH

By the summer of 1913, Grimké was an author, orator, diplomat, attorney and a youthful-looking sixty-four years. Tall and elegant with silver-white hair and a trim moustache to match, he had an aristocratic look that commanded respect, and his serious demeanor indicated a no-nonsense approach to all matters. He was more than qualified to replace Waldron, but the board of directors did not select him immediately.[92]

With Waldron now gone, Villard wanted to go further than Mary White Ovington's memorandum that the branch have an advisory committee composed of "majority white men." Why not have a white man take the branch presidency? On September 12, he offered the position to his friend, Moses Clapp, a liberal Republican senator from Minnesota. Although Villard praised the branch as "a fine group there, including the most representative colored people," he exaggerated the necessity of white support: "Never before have the colored people in Washington been in such desperate

U.S. senator Moses Clapp of Minnesota (*right*) was offered the presidency of the branch by Oswald Garrison Villard after John Milton Waldron's removal in September 1913. Believing it would be a conflict of interest, Clapp did not accept. *Library of Congress (LC-DIG-hec-00465).*

need of influential white friends." The request to the senator was a stark contradiction given Villard's opposition to Waldron's dalliance with politics. But Clapp recognized the conflict of interest and declined the offer; as a senator, he did not want to lead an organization that was likely to affect (and be affected) by congressional action.[93]

THE BRANCH FIGHTS THE PRESIDENT

Nerney put Grimké over the top. She had made several trips to Washington that summer to investigate reports of segregation practices in the federal government. Nerney liked Grimké personally, despised Waldron, and so, upon her return to New York, she urged the national body to appoint him temporary branch president until an election could be held for a permanent replacement in January 1914. Local activists also encouraged Grimké to take the position. He finally agreed in late September. There was a lot of work to do, but Grimké believed that segregation could galvanize the branch. Wilson made that task easy both for him and the national office. The organization had launched a mass protest campaign on August 15 with a stinging letter to Wilson that criticized the policies, outlined their harm and noted that Black employees working behind screens and closed doors "as if they were leprous" had "the badge of inferiority pressed upon them by Government decree." It was circulated broadly: congressional offices, the press and NAACP branches. The strategy to garner attention to the injustice worked. With the exception of the South, harsh editorials against the administration appeared in newspapers all over the country. Branches from Boston to Denver coordinated protests and sent thousands of signed resolutions to members of Congress and the president.[94]

Words on paper from prominent civil rights officials who condemned segregation were powerful, but had no effect on Wilson, especially when these writers were not experiencing it themselves. It was time for the president to hear directly from people who actually were confined to these segregated workplaces. Grimké attempted a different tactic, one that demonstrated he was willing to make the branch utilize confrontation and advocate on behalf of working-class residents, a group that did not exclusively comprise the membership. He gathered twenty-five Post Office employees who relished the opportunity to express their grievances to Wilson. He informed Villard of his plan with the belief that if the president was willing to yield time for a delegation of white women from New Jersey demanding suffrage rights, he was obligated to grant that same courtesy to Black workers. Grimké was more determined to put the group in front of Wilson when some told him they wished for their president's "New Freedom" to also apply to their jobs and livelihoods.[95]

Villard managed to please and disappoint Grimké at the same time. He embraced the plan but urged Grimké to ensure that the delegation's approach in the Oval Office would be "moderate in expression." Grimké thought the request was unnecessary, but it did not matter anyway. Wilson declined the meeting and still had not budged by early October. Segregation, the president believed, was "a rational, scientific policy," and devoid of racism. "It is as far as possible from being a movement against the negroes. I sincerely believe it to be in their best interest." However, Wilson confided privately to Villard, who was finally able to meet with him in early October, that he had failed this test of leadership: "I have thought about this thing for twenty years and I see no way out. It will take a very big man to solve this thing."[96]

On October 27, the branch held a mass meeting at Metropolitan AME against segregation—or "The New Slavery"—as it was advertised. The venue was symbolic; the branch was organized there and was less than a mile from the White House. Two thousand people filled the church. Due to the crowd, John Jay Holmes, a Unitarian minister from New York and one of the main speakers, had to be lifted over a fence in order to enter the building through a side entrance. After the Howard University choir opened the meeting with a rendition of "By the Waters of Babylon," Villard fired up the audience by announcing he would never do what the White House proposed: keep "the colored people in a cool and just equipoise." He would work with Grimké "to preach the doctrine of peaceful rebellion and revolution against discrimination of any kind." Finally, it was Grimké's turn to speak. In remarks titled "Honor or Dishonor," he ripped into Wilson, accusing him of abandoning his campaign pledges of equality and justice. "My friends…we feel…as if we have been betrayed by a trusted friend into the hands of our bitterest enemies." The membership adopted a stinging resolution condemning federal segregation: *"That this insult to the colored people of this country is resented and we enter our vigorous protest against it to the President of the United States"* and elbowed Wilson by dispatching it to the White House two days later with a letter from Grimké informing him that he had also sent copies "to the Secretary of the Treasury and to the Post Master General."[97]

For weeks, the Metropolitan gathering was referred to as "the great meeting" all over Black Washington. The branch now had a cause to fight

Archibald Grimké with the branch's "Committee of Forty." It raised funds for the campaign against the Wilson administration's segregation of the federal workforce. *Library of Congress.*

for, but money was vital to sustain the battle. Grimké created a "Committee of Fifty" to raise funds; members were required to pledge or donate $25. He also created a speakers' bureau to spread the word about the branch's work and goals. No place would be excluded. Whether a church, societal organization, business or lodge, the bureau was instructed to go everywhere "until they reached everyone and everyone was willing to give something." One teacher organized a group of his students to contribute a dime a week until they reached $35, making them "full" members. Du Bois reported in *The Crisis* that the branch "has reached the people." By the end of the year, membership increased from 143 to 700, and $2,500 had been sent to the national office. It was now the largest branch in the country.[98]

The branch was fighting segregation against the administration and Congress, but glimmers of hope emerged in this bilateral war. Several members quietly investigated reports of discrimination and kept whistleblowers' identities confidential. Some inquiries were encouraging. In November 1913, Grimké learned that Black clerks in the Treasury Department's Sixth Auditor's Office rejoined their white colleagues. This was not a cause for celebration, he cautioned. Until no department was segregated, the NAACP could not claim victory. By the end of the year, the national office was pleased with Grimké's work and elected him vice president of the association, which included an appointment to the board of directors. He was optimistic about the mission that lay ahead. "We must shake this country by agitation," he declared in an address to the national office. "We have set a torch, we have lighted it, we have applied it to the republic, and all the wickedness, all the wrong, will finally be burnt of it, if it takes fifty or seventy-five years."[99]

The membership was revitalized too. In a display of strong support, Grimké was elected president in January 1914. He became a constant presence on Capitol Hill for the entire year, often showing up at committee hearings to offer testimony against Jim Crow legislation, angering lawmakers but delighting the branch and national headquarters. "It is most unfortunate… that the colored people are obliged to come before a committee and ask you not to humiliate them," he told the House Committee on Civil Service and Reform. At first, Grimké assumed a strikingly accommodationist position like that of Booker T. Washington. Black people had proved their loyalty to white people in the antebellum South as slaves and now were doing so as servants in the federal government. Therefore, it was unfair for them to be discriminated against. "Let them alone," he told the committee.[100]

The legislators attempted to undermine his credibility and tarnish him as a partisan causing unnecessary consternation over an issue that did not even merit a discussion. What was his political affiliation? they asked. Grimké responded that he had supported Democrats, Republicans and Progressives during his life. Did he even know how the Black community in Washington felt about segregation? "Yes sir, they are objecting to it," he stated. Would any Black employee in the District desire segregation? "I have never heard of any," the NAACP leader replied with conviction. What gave him the right to speak before them as a representative of the Black race? they demanded. "I have the blood of both races," Grimké retorted matter-of-factly. He then abandoned the Washingtonian approach, especially after several congressmen, like Martin Dies of Texas, resorted to the usual call for white rule and dominance: "We have solved the question of the South and white supremacy is a fixture." "You think you have solved it, but you cannot do it," Grimké shot back. "You cannot separate the colored people in the Government service without humiliating them. Separation always means inequality."[101]

As the NAACP's representative in the capital, the branch and the national office developed a well-coordinated strategy to defeat such legislation.

Several journalists were hired to cover Grimké's encounters on the Hill and reported to Nerney, who, in turn, compiled bulletins about congressional action and distributed them to other branches throughout the country. She also submitted the reports to Du Bois, who published them in *The Crisis*. The resistance worked. Congress adjourned without passing a single piece of anti-Black legislation on March 4, 1915. On the Jim Crow streetcar bills specifically, the branch mounted pressure on the House District of Columbia Committee to skip "District Day" when Congress devoted one day to focus on local affairs, which effectively killed the legislation.[102]

The branch's campaign against these segregation proposals was the first example of its jockeying between conservatism and confrontational direct action. In this instance, it chose the latter. The mass meeting at Metropolitan, Grimké's attempt for an Oval Office face-off with Wilson and his plan to put working-class postal workers in front of the president connected with Black Washingtonians. However, as aggressive as the movement was, it was still imperfect. Branch members did not picket in front of the White House and the U.S. Capitol or attempt sit-in demonstrations in lawmakers' offices. Its leaders also did not encourage the Black community to engage in these actions.

THE BIRTH OF A NATION

The branch soon faced a new challenge: the power of racist cinematic propaganda. On February 18, 1915, David Wark Griffith, a Kentucky-born actor who had a remarkable flair for transforming a scrappy nickel-and-dime business into an astounding art of storytelling as a director and producer, lugged his suitcases through Union Station. Inside were twelve movie reels. Thomas Dixon Jr., a friend and former Johns Hopkins University classmate of Wilson's, had adapted his 1905 novel and play *The Clansman: A Historical Romance of the Ku Klux Klan* into a film. *The Clansman* had premiered at the Clune Auditorium in Riverside, California, two weeks before and was met with protest by the Los Angeles NAACP. Griffith and Dixon were granted permission to show the film at a private White House screening. The director was giddy. His last time in the city was 1907, when his play *A Fool and a Girl* bombed at the Columbia Theatre, but now it was thrilling that a president would be in his audience.[103]

"It is like writing history with lightning. And my only regret is that it is all so terribly true," Wilson reportedly said at its conclusion. Many

D.W. Griffith with actresses Dorothy and Lillian Gish at the White House. Despite protests, the branch failed to prevent *The Birth of a Nation* from playing in Washington. *Library of Congress (LC-DIG-hec-42074).*

historians debate the authenticity of those two sentences, but the applause that filled the East Room when the lights came on led Dixon and Griffith, both ardent self-promoters, to claim that *The Clansman* had received a presidential seal of approval.[104]

The Los Angeles NAACP's failure to prevent *The Clansman*'s showing changed the method that the national office and District branch approached the racist production. The LA censorship board had approved the chapter's request to ban the film, but Griffith circumvented action by obtaining a court injunction against future interferences with its showing. In March, with a New York City premiere approaching, Dixon urged Griffith to drop the title in favor of one that was less biting and more uplifting: *The Birth of a Nation.* Spingarn appealed to the National Board of Censorship (NBC) to withdraw its original support. It was a fragmented victory: the divided board agreed to delete certain scenes but refused to ban the film entirely, claiming its authority centered on moral content, not historical accuracy. Furthermore, it concluded that since the motion picture industry was not art, censorship was not applicable as it violated First Amendment protections. Any battle to defeat *Birth* now rested on the shoulders of NAACP branches working with local officials and organizations. Spingarn instructed all chapters to "immediately interest the local clergy, colored and white, civic organizations, welfare societies, women's clubs, etc. to unite with you in a protest."[105]

Protests against *Birth* continued nationally. An effort to bring the film to Washington was noticed by W.A. Adams, owner of the Adams Sheet Music House at 1005 U Street NW in early February 1916. He read in the *Star* that the Sons of Confederate Veterans' "Camp 305 was appointed to co-operate" with Maude Howell of the District chapter of the United Daughters of the Confederacy (UDC) "in bringing to Washington the motion picture." Adams sent the clipping and a brief letter not to the branch but to Du Bois so he would publish it in *The Crisis* and also because "I trust the Washington branch may be fully informed thereof."[106]

It was indeed. George William Cook had urged Grimké to take action in October 1915. There was no mayor for the branch to appeal to, but there were the District commissioners, the police chief and Wilson. Cook wanted Grimké to organize delegations to call for these powerful individuals to ban the film. Soliciting participation would not be a problem; the branch now had an army of 1,500 members. Cook targeted Wilson, who attempted to duck the controversy completely. "Its exhibition at the White House was a courtesy extended to an old acquaintance" was the official White House statement. The delegations, Cook reasoned, were the perfect opportunity to force Wilson to finally either embrace or reject *Birth* altogether. "Whether we could keep The Birth of a Nation out of Washington or not, it will at least show we have some sensibilities," he wrote.[107]

In late February 1916, the branch's monthly meeting at Lincoln was devoted entirely to *Birth*. Notices described a "film which stirs up race hatred," asked "What is our Branch going to do?" and invited "a full discussion as a basis for vigorous action." To members, Wilson's stance that the screening was just a favor for a friend was ludicrous. His own quotations were featured in *Birth*, which indicated the event was tantamount to a presidential endorsement of the film. After several ideas were circulated, a member suggested a radical solution. If all else failed, then the chemists of the city, of which he was one, "should get together and prevent the showing of the play by the use of explosives," according to the *Afro American*.[108]

Grimké rejected that idea and insisted the branch would not resort to the resistance tactics of a "black hand" organization. He also called the dissidents' bluff by remarking that individuals who announced such action would never carry it out themselves. The *Afro* editorialized that the "Washington Branch is to be congratulated on having a level headed president" but still endorsed the idea of bombing the venue where *Birth* would open in the city. There was a time when violence was appropriate "when every other means has failed." Nat Turner's insurrection against slavery in Virginia in 1831 and John Brown's Harpers Ferry raid had proven that. The chemist's suggestion was "a splendid idea," but if carried out, would be representative not only of the branch but also of "the nine thousand members outside of the District of Columbia who had no part in it."[109]

With *Birth*'s debut now inevitable, the national office decided to counter the film with productions that would educate audiences about the Black experience and place them in a positive context. In 1911, Du Bois produced *The Star of Ethiopia*, a five-scene play about "the rise and development of the Negro race" that covers both the might of ancient Egypt and other civilizations and "a weakened Africa which fell prey to Christian slave traders." The first production opened in New York in 1913, but Du Bois brought it to Washington specifically as a rallying cry against *Birth* in October 1915, when it was presented with "one thousand actors" at Griffith Stadium. "The one idea that dominates the whole is that the Negro has a past of which he should we proud," the *Afro* stated in a powerful review.[110]

Inspired by *Ethiopia*, the branch's Drama Committee followed suit in early March 1916 with a three-act play titled *Rachel* written by Grimké's daughter, Angelina, and produced by Clifford, Anna Julia Cooper and Howard University educator and philosopher Alain Locke. Described in its playbill as "the first attempt to use the stage for race propaganda in order to enlighten the American people relative to the lamentable condition of millions of colored citizens in this free Republic," it tells a melancholy story of Black womanhood and family. Although not as uplifting as *Ethiopia*, it rejects the falsehoods and distortions in *Birth*. It also would later serve as a model in the anti-lynching literary movement in the 1920s, as the character Rachel rejects motherhood after the deaths of her father and brother from mob violence. Tickets were sold at Gray and Gray's Drug Store at Twelfth and U Streets NW, and *Rachel* opened at the Miner Normal School in which "a capacity audience was in attendance," according to a *Star* review. "The participants were uniformly excellent. Miss Rachel Guy in the role of Rachel, the leading character, displayed talent in a part that necessitated considerable range and ability along emotional lines."[111]

The branch made a final pitch when Grimké requested a hearing before the District Commissioners, who had the authority to stop the film. Footage of Black

The branch's Drama Committee countered the racism of *The Birth of a Nation* with *Rachel*, a three-act play about Black womanhood and family. It was written by Archibald Grimké's daughter, Angelina. *Moorland-Spingarn Research Center, Howard University.*

heavyweight boxing legend Jack Johnson's 1910 victory over his white opponent, James Jeffries, had been prohibited from display for six years by the commissioners, who feared that the riots it sparked in other parts of the country would erupt in the District. For them to permit *Birth's* showing, which had evoked the same reaction elsewhere, would be hypocritical, Grimké wrote. The branch also appealed to Republican members of Congress who introduced bills instructing the commissioners to ban the film. Missouri representative Leonidas C. Dyer, who allied himself with the NAACP to pass anti-lynching legislation in the 1920s, put forth a measure to the House Committee on Interstate and Foreign Commerce that fined any person who brought the film into the District "not more than $1,000 or sentenced to imprisonment at hard labor for not more than one year, or both at the discretion of the court." However, the bill died in committee, along with two others similar in scope.[112]

The commissioners denied Grimké's request, and the film opened at the National Theater on April 17. Tickets sold out quickly due to the hype the city's white newspapers provided. "Last night's capacity audience…indicated a full appreciation of the art, the truth, and the dramatic power of a historical spectacle than which no theatrical entertainment in recent years has had a surer or more potent appeal," the *Post* reported the next day.[113]

Grimké was flustered. Even the branch's desire to slow its popularity and minimize attendance resulted in no consensus on how to accomplish that goal. A local artist, "Mr. Portlock," created an anti-*Birth* cartoon but needed money from the branch to publish it. Believing it would only arouse Washingtonians' curiosity and compel them even more to go see the film, Grimké denied the funds. *Birth* also had another unexpected consequence. Emboldened by the film's content, another wave of anti-Black legislation engulfed the Sixty-Fourth Congress. Defeat was never final with these bills; they were always introduced repeatedly or attached to legislative packages

as amendments. Once again, Grimké found himself on the Hill speaking against efforts to bring segregated streetcars and anti-intermarriage laws to the city. In the Senate, James Reed of Missouri inserted a proposal excluding "all Members of the African or Black Race" into a major immigration bill. It narrowly passed the upper chamber 29 to 25, but pressure from the branch led to its defeat (and all the others) in the House by a 252 to 75 vote. NAACP secretary Roy Nash consoled Grimké on the branch's split victory of not preventing *Birth*'s debut but torpedoing Jim Crow legislation in Congress: "Of course, the fight was well worth making regardless of outcome. As far as effective protest goes, however, we have pretty near shot our bolt."[114]

That was not true. The radical elements within the branch were silenced by the majority of members who espoused more conservative approaches to banning the film. Although bombing the venue where *Birth* would debut

NEW NATIONAL THEATRE

DIRECTION   W.H.RAPLEY

BUSINESS MANAGEMENT   W.H.FOWLER

Week Commencing Sunday, May 14, 1916—Matinees Daily

D. W. GRIFFITH Presents

THE BIRTH OF A NATION

An Historical Drama in Two Acts.

NOTE.—There will be an intermission of eight minutes between Acts I and II.

CAST OF CHARACTERS

COL. BEN CAMERON	HENRY WALTHALL
MARGARET CAMERON, the Elder Sister	MIRIAM COOPER
FLORA, the Pet Sister	MAE MARSH
MRS. CAMERON	JOSEPHINE CROWELL
DR. CAMERON	SPOTTISWOODE AIKEN
WADE CAMERON, the Second Son	J. A. BERINGER
DUKE CAMERON, the Youngest Son	MAXFIELD STANLEY
MAMMY, Their Faithful Old Servant	JENNIE LEE
HON. AUSTIN STONEMAN, Leader of the House	RALPH LEWIS
ELSIE, His Daughter	LILLIAN GISH
PHIL, His Elder Son	ELMER CLIFTON
TOD, the Younger Son	ROBERT HARRON
JEFF, the Blacksmith	WALLACE REED
LYDIA BROWN, Stoneman's Mulatto Housekeeper	MARY ALDEN
SILAS LYNCH, Mulatto Lieutenant Governor	GEORGE SEIGMANN
GUS, a Renegade Negro	WALTER LONG
ABRAHAM LINCOLN	JOSEPH HENABERY
JOHN WILKES BOOTH	RAOUL WALSH
GEN. U. S. GRANT	DONALD CRISP
GEN. ROBT. E. LEE	HOWARD GAYE
NELSE, an Old-Fashioned Negro	WILLIAM DE VAULL
JAKE, a Black Man Faithful Unto Death	WILLIAM FREEMAN
STONEMAN'S SERVANT	THOMAS WILSON

Cabinet Members, Generals, Military Aides and Attaches, Secretaries, Senators, Representatives, Visitors, Soldiers, Abolitionists, Ku Klux Klansmen, Plantation Crowds and Mobs.

(Continued on page 11)

Opposite: *The Birth of a Nation* premiered in Washington at the New National Theater on April 17, 1916, and played there for five weeks. *DC Public Library.*

Above: *The Birth of a Nation* advertisement in a New National Theater playbill. *DC Public Library.*

was immediately dismissed as an act of terrorism, the branch still did not engage in the confrontational, nonviolent protests that others in the country utilized that yielded some victories over Griffith's racist masterpiece. Pickets prevented openings of *Birth* in Gary, Indiana, Boston and all of Ohio. In Oakland, California, and St. Paul, Minnesota, branches forced theaters to delete certain scenes. The Tacoma, Washington branch secured the passage of legislation that prohibited the showing of racist productions altogether.[115]

In contrast, the D.C. branch did not adopt those methods. For all the desire to pressure Wilson to reject the film, there were no pickets in front of the White House, as suffragists had done in 1913. There were no demonstrations at the District Building, which housed the commissioners' offices. Throughout the country, NAACP branches picketed the theaters where *Birth* was shown. In Washington, the branch initiated no protests outside the National Theater during the film's five-week run. Lobbying, letter-writing campaigns and the courts were considered more viable solutions by the Black elite membership than civil disobedience in the streets. That cautious philosophy was exemplified in Waldron's response after the commissioners approved the film. The pastor, who headed a *Birth* protest committee, signaled legal action when he emphasized "we will not violate the law but intend to go as far as possible within the law to accomplish this end. For the branch, direct, confrontational protests were a violation of the law."[116]

"Red Summer" in D.C.

By the end of World War I, the membership had soared to more than five thousand, a goal the national office wanted. Grimké wrote to Moorfield Storey in 1918, acknowledging past problems that had dragged time and attention from important work. The branch was now beyond its infancy stages, and Grimké at last believed he was the leader "not of a handful of radicals…but of a coherent group of substantial citizens, representing all elements of our local population." In June 1919, he attended the annual meeting in Chicago. He was bestowed the Spingarn Medal, the association's most prestigious award, for "seventy years of distinguished service to his country and his Race" and for his branch leadership to "safeguard of the rights of 11,000,000 people at the Capital." Members were elated, but the *Afro American*, which had provided Grimké and the branch's work with favorable coverage as a staunch ally, rebuked the choice as an "unpopular selection." Up until that year, the medal had gone to an individual who had done stellar work for the betterment of the race and was not an NAACP member or officer. The association's citation of Grimké's branch presidency as the main reason for the award was an alarming conflict of interest, and he did not deserve it, the *Afro* editorialized. "Many…will not agree that Mr. Grimké has made the highest achievement among his race during the last half century."[117]

Nevertheless, Grimké did not have much time to bask in the glow of his medal. In July, he wrote letters to House Speaker Frederick Gillette and Michigan representative (and House District of Columbia Committee chairman) Carl Mapes regarding the Senate's restaurant policy of not serving Black patrons. The ink had barely dried when the city erupted into several incidents of racial violence that were part of what NAACP assistant secretary James Weldon Johnson called "Red Summer" in reference to the bloodshed. In February, the city welcomed the Second First Battalion of the National Guard home from Europe with a jubilant parade down Pennsylvania Avenue. Two hundred soldiers from the all-Black unit had perished on the battlefields of France, including thirty from the District. By July, the decoration for their bravery was old news as the capital faced housing and work shortages with civilians, soldiers and an influx of migrants competing for jobs and opportunity. Additionally, the city's four major dailies were publishing stories of predatory assaults on white women by a mysterious Black rapist, stoking white fears about the taboo of interracial sex. On July 9, the branch wrote to the editors, warning that their sensational and inflammatory headlines were "sowing the seeds of a race riot" by "featuring 'Negro' in all sorts of unnecessary ways." Only the *Star* acknowledged "the justice of the Association's complaint. The other papers ignored our warning," an open letter to members said.[118]

On Friday, July 18, an incident involving Elsie Stephnick, a nineteen-year-old white woman who worked at the Bureau of Engraving and Printing at Fourteenth and B Streets NW (now Independence Avenue), triggered what the *New York Times* dubbed "The Race War in Washington." Two Black men reportedly accosted her as she walked to her home in Southwest at 10:00 p.m. after completing her shift. She escaped harm; they fled when she screamed. Word spread quickly to her husband, John, and his friends and colleagues at the Naval Aviation Service. The police questioned Charles Ralls, a Black resident of the Bloodfield neighborhood in Southwest and a person of interest, and released him, but Williams became convinced that he was one of the attackers. At 10:30 p.m. on Saturday, a mob of military servicemen, some in uniform, gathered at Seventh and Pennsylvania Avenues NW, then crossed into Bloodfield. The crowd found Ralls and his wife, beating several along the way, and attacked them. However, the couple was able to escape. Neighbors intervened and fended off the mob, which then attempted to invade the Ralls home. Police made no arrests.[119]

And so it had begun. The mob grew larger on Sunday night. By then, the branch believed the situation warranted the intervention of the military and requested that Navy Secretary Josephus Daniels and War Secretary Newton Baker "take action to restrain [those]…who were responsible for Saturday night's disturbances" and "punish the guilty and to prevent a recurrence of the performance." Daniels did nothing, but Baker ordered white soldiers from as far as Quantico, Virginia, into the city to restore order. Meanwhile, very few places were safe for Black Washingtonians from the knives, guns, clubs and sticks the mob carried to unleash their fury. Two men were beaten in front of the White House. Seventeen-year-old Francis Thomas was almost killed after being attacked on the Seventh Street streetcar and thrown through one of its open windows. A Black man collapsed in front of the palatial Raleigh Hotel after a vicious assault. Others were attacked outside the Washington Post Building and Carnegie Library. Noted historian Carter G. Woodson narrowly escaped death when he encountered a mob at the corner of Eighth Street NW. He ran in the other direction after shots rang out, and the crowd pursued another victim.[120]

The branch requested Navy Secretary Josephus Daniels take action to stop white military servicemen from attacking African Americans during the "Red Summer" riot in Washington. *Library of Congress (LC-USZ62-96840).*

War Secretary Newton Baker complied with the branch's demand to use military action to quell the violence during "Red Summer" and ordered white soldiers from as far as Quantico, Virginia, into the city. *Library of Congress (LC-DIG-npcc-20090).*

The branch also turned to city officials. Thomas, along with attorneys James Cobb, William L. Houston and F.S. Phillips—who comprised the Legal Committee—met with Louis Brownlow, president of the D.C. commissioners, and Police Chief Raymond Pullman "and urged that they take effective action to prevent assaults upon defenseless colored people who were the victims of the attacks." The violence forced bitter enemies in the branch to set aside their differences; Waldron organized a committee of local pastors to support Thomas's delegation. Informed by Brownlow about the arrival of troops, the group demanded to know why Black soldiers were not included. Brownlow dodged the question but insisted that white rioters would be arrested and fairness would prevail in the resolution of the conflict. Unconvinced, Thomas led the group out of the meeting.[121]

Baker was not the only one mobilizing forces. The *Post* resorted to its own call for reinforcements at "9 o'clock and the purpose of a 'clean-up' that will cause the events of the last two evenings to pale into insignificance." Alarmed that the press was provoking attacks, Black Washingtonians defended their homes, neighborhoods and families. Black residents circumvented local gun dealers' refusal to sell ammunition by driving to Baltimore to smuggle firearms. Some Black war veterans simply used the weaponry they had when they returned from Europe. Neighborhood patrols were set up, and snipers

Above: Attorneys James Cobb, Perry Howard and George E.C. Hayes (*left to right*), representing the branch's Legal Committee, successfully reduced Black defendants' jail sentences to probations. *Moorland-Spingarn Research Center, Howard University.*

Left: Branch leaders met with Louis Brownlow (*right*), president of the District commissioners, to urge action to stop the violence in the city. Brownlow later revealed privately to NAACP executive secretary James Weldon Johnson that white anger at Black Washingtonians played a role in the attacks. *Library of Congress (LC-DIG-hec-25072).*

took defensive positions atop the roof of the Howard Theater in anticipation of the invaders. Their actions reflected what the branch delegation told Brownlow and Pullman. They had "determined not to stand up and be shot down like dogs, but they were prepared to protect their families and would do so at all hazard." Many were arrested for what Pullman called "gun play." Thomas saw two thousand Black defenders on Florida Avenue and U Street from Sixth to Fourteenth Streets. Walking through the area, he told Grimké with pride that their presence indicated "their purpose to die for their race and defy the white mob."[122]

The violence finally ended on July 22 after Wilson, sick with acute diarrhea and anxious over the fate of the Treaty of Versailles to bring peace to a war-weary world, finally mobilized the National Guard. Six people were killed, and many more suffered fractured skulls and kneecaps, gunshot wounds, broken jaws and an array of other bloody lacerations. Blame for the riot varied among the media and law enforcement. One consensus was that there was no single cause. The *Post* blamed "hoodlums of all colors" and the police. The *New York Times* singled out officers but also indicted "exasperated" white vigilantes and a "criminal element among the negroes." Brownlow privately revealed to Johnson, who arrived in the District from New York on Monday night, that white anger at Black Washingtonians'

may have played a role in the attacks. Grimké received letters from other branches offering assistance, but distrustful of the information coming out of Washington, they wanted the truth. George Vaughn, an attorney and executive committee member of the St. Louis, Missouri branch, asked him "to send him facts." Dr. J.J. Robinson, president of the Providence, Rhode Island branch, posed three questions: "Are the Negroes the only persons in Washington who are drinking the bad whiskey as they claim?" "Is it absolutely certain that these assaults on white women were not made by men of their own race blacked up?" "Were the sailors, soldiers, and marines stationed around Washington southern men?"[123]

Attorney General Alexander Mitchell Palmer refused a request from the branch to prosecute the *Washington Post* for inciting violence with its inflammatory headlines during "Red Summer." *Library of Congress (LC-DIG-ds-07209).*

Anger in the District's Black community ran deep with the *Post*'s role in instigating the mob violence, particularly the "clean-up" headline. Calls to hold the newspaper accountable prompted the branch to send a letter to Attorney General Alexander Mitchell Palmer requesting that he authorize the Justice Department to charge the *Post* with inciting a riot. The department rejected the request, citing no grounds for action. However, the branch had more success—through its legal committee—in court with the dozens of Black self-defenders who had been jailed and beaten in the station houses for carrying weapons. Cobb, Houston and Royal Hughes, a young attorney described by branch secretary Swan Kendrick as "enthusiastic and eager" to offer counsel to anyone who desired it, reduced the sentences of all the defendants in Police Court to brief probations.[124]

A "New Negro" Identity

The 1913–19 period was one of the most tumultuous in the history of the branch. As one of the NAACP's earliest branches, it bore the unique distinction of becoming precariously close to extinction so briefly after it had formed. Its resurrection was a resounding defeat to the implicit bias from the national office that white male leadership was essential to its survival. For its members, the success in derailing the most hostile legislation targeting Black Washingtonians compensated for the failure to slay the dragon of Wilsonian segregation. The branch was grateful for Grimké's leadership and never again placed an emphasis on the trivial celebrity that had doomed Waldron. He answered inquiries from other branches seeking advice on wide-ranging matters. Some had nothing to do with civil rights. One week before the Red Summer violence, Fred Morton, principal of the Manassas Industrial School for Colored Youth in Virginia, wrote to Grimké as one of the final candidates for the presidency of the West Virginia Collegiate Institute in Charleston. He requested a letter from Grimké "endorsing my moral Fitness for the work." In October, Thomas Redd, a member of the Louisville, Kentucky branch, sought Grimké's help in finding a family in the city who was willing to rent a room to his son, James, who was unable to secure housing as an incoming Howard University freshman. Grimké came through for both men.[125]

However, for all the D.C. branch's success, there was also criticism that induced some soul-searching. Woodson argued that a lack of a central meeting place or headquarters hindered the branch's outreach to the Black community. Hosting meetings at many of the city's churches, schools, the YMCA and the YWCA was not strategically wise because it gave the organization the illusion of erraticism. He offered to pay the first month's rent on a permanent headquarters if the executive committee would secure a venue. It was rejected, not because it was unreasonable, but because it came with a catch. Woodson also advocated the branch divide up the city's Black neighborhoods into twenty-five districts with one agent presiding over each area. "Through these agents, meetings of importance, our urgent needs and the general welfare of the race will be kept before every Negro in the city," he told Grimké. Woodson also called for these agents to draw "patronage from business establishments which do not treat both races alike." The implication was clear; Woodson envisioned supporting only Black businesses and boycotting white establishments. It generated controversy within the ranks, as many members, including Grimké, believed such militancy would bring retaliatory lawsuits from the white community. So be it, Woodson argued. Welcoming such action "would do the cause much good." Woodson's priority was not increasing membership rosters and *Crisis* subscriptions but to "get the support of all the colored business men of the city and use their stores as a militant center." As a "radical," there was "no other way of getting the work of the National Association for the Advancement of Colored People permanently attached to the community."[126]

Woodson's sentiments embodied the sense of militancy that characterized Black Washington after the riot. A more resistant and assertive "new Negro" identity had emerged, one that was now more unwilling than ever to bow to white subjugation. In the aftermath of Washington's race war, Mary Church Terrell wrote that the "general slaughter of Negroes...won't be suffered any longer" and Black residents showed "that Washington has awakened and I'm glad of it." Waldron brought his 350-member congregation to their feet at Shiloh on the Sunday after the turmoil when he declared "we are dealing with a new negro and not with the old slave." What had instilled pride in Black Washingtonians angered many of their white neighbors. In a District restaurant, a visitor from Alabama told Joseph Manning, a native southerner covering affairs in the city as a *Cleveland Gazette* reporter: "I am astonished at the resistance put up by these Washington niggers. These folk will have to find some other way to teach them their place."[127]

That militancy percolated quietly in the branch but never surfaced. Grimké was held in high regard as an elder statesman, but he was intolerant of radicalism, as evidenced by his methods to prevent *Birth*'s showing and assurance to Storey that he was not the leader of a militant organization. The next decade in Washington necessitated a radical direction. Neval Thomas had made a name for himself in the city and within the branch and the national office. The manner in which African Americans handled themselves "was one of reprisal but it was effective, and pursued with beautiful purpose and self-sacrifice," he said after Red Summer. In the Roaring Twenties, Thomas would attempt to awaken that sleeping giant within the branch.[128]

4

"DON'T LET THE KU KLUX CATCH YOU NAPPING!"

The branch leadership had applied both activist and moderate-conservative protest tactics to the conflicts it faced in the 1910s. However, radicalism in its leadership and among its members would be the strongest in the latter half of the 1920s under Neval Thomas.

Although his branch presidency was inevitable, it was not immediate. The Springfield, Ohio native had proven to be a leader in his own right in the 1910s but especially in the waning days of 1919. That autumn, while Grimké grappled with the aftermath of Red Summer and Jim Crowism in the Senate restaurant, Thomas battled segregation in similar quarters at the D.C. Supreme Court. He sent numerous letters to Chief Justice Walter McCoy and Justice Stafford about the conditions in their building. A "three-day siege" (as Thomas described his lone sit-in demonstration to Mary White Ovington), aided by coverage in the *Washington Eagle*, a small, Black, radical newspaper, finally led to the restaurant's desegregation of its Black employees and removal of restrictions against Black patrons. Ovington responded with warm congratulations and asked for his advice to successfully end the Jim Crow practices in the Library of Congress restaurant since she was getting the runaround from lawmakers: "Tell us just what to do in regard to the Library restaurant. The Committee chairman to who we wrote…replied that the Library officials were presidential appointees." Wilson had been contacted, she said, "but [we] have received no reply from him yet." Grimké was never consulted.[129]

Neval Thomas's "three-day siege" of the DC Supreme Court's segregated restaurant led to the removal of its Jim Crow policies in the autumn of 1919. *DC Public Library.*

The 1920s did begin with a self-described "militant" at the branch's helm, but in name only. The national NAACP's constitution granted the executive secretary significant power, and the branches were no exception. The position, held by Shelby Davidson, exerted a dominant role in the organizational structure. Born in 1868 in Lexington, Kentucky, Davidson came to Washington to attend Howard University. Upon graduation in 1893, he secured work in the federal government as an unclassified laborer and also studied law at Howard. A clerk's position became available at the Treasury Department's Auditor of the Post Office where Davidson expertly invented devices for tabulating and totaling accounts, compiling money order reports for postmasters and coin machine tabulation. Despite his talents, he encountered intense racial discrimination in the department and launched a personal crusade against it even before Wilson's policies came into fruition. Realizing that his civil rights work would be strengthened with legal experience, Davidson ended his government career in 1912 and became devoted to his law practice and real estate business full-time. By the time Wilson was elected, Davidson was admitted to the bar in the District and Kentucky and qualified to argue cases before the Supreme Court.[130]

Optimism in the new decade felt wonderful. In April 1920, the officers distributed *What the Branch Has Done*, a pamphlet of "the efforts and accomplishments" that summarized victories in civil service, courts, race riots, schools, and segregation "during the year 1919" and laid out plans to continue the progress. No member who possessed a copy could not feel prideful; it reminded them they were members of an effective and important branch. And for those Black Washingtonians who were not, a subliminal message lay therein: come and join the fight.[131]

One glorious reality in particular was that Woodrow Wilson was no longer president, as the *Afro-American* jubilantly reminded its readers on March 4, 1921: "Woodrow Wilson leaves the White House today, with the praise of his successor ringing in his ears, and with the ill-will and disfavor of his fellow countrymen. No President of the United States has been so unpopular and so thoroly [sic] hated in the history of the nation." The new Republican president, Warren Harding, spoke of "an era of good feeling" in his inaugural address and promised an end to federal workplace segregation and discrimination. Such oratory provided hope for that era of good feeling; perhaps the branch could commit to combating racism elsewhere in the city instead of federal executive departments. This would not be the case, but the branch did address such issues. The Committee on Schools and Legislation raised "between one-fourth and one-third" of all the funds appropriated for the District's "colored schools which has not been practiced heretofore." The branch also successfully added several African Americans to the city's police force "and assisted materially in the…setting up of a complete colored fire company," although it was segregated. In 1921, the branch, pleased with its work, reported to attendees of the twelfth annual convention in Detroit that it "was in one of the most prosperous and healthy conditions of any year since its organization."[132]

By spring 1922, Davidson had greatly impressed the national office. In late March, James Weldon Johnson read a letter from him, elated at some news from Washington. Plans for the District, Virginia and Maryland chapters of the Ku Klux Klan to "assemble at the Virginia end of one of the bridges," enter and parade through the capital, then head back to Alexandria had been foiled by the executive secretary.[133]

Founded on January 1, 1921, the District's Klan chapter was headquartered in the Munsey Building office of Harry Terrell, an attorney and the "grand goblin of the Capital Domain, Realm of the District of Columbia." "A pleasant, smooth-shaven man of forty years," as the *Star* described him, Terrell claimed the chapter, numbering "several hundred," was not violent.

"We do not engage in night riding," he told a *Star* reporter. It was simply a patriotic organization—for "the native-born white American citizens who believe in the tenets of the Christian religion." Law enforcement was on his group's side, Terrell boasted. "The chief of police here would find the members…willing to assist…authorities and maintain law and order."[134]

The bond with D.C. Police major Daniel Sullivan was not as solid as Terrell thought. By 1922, Klan activity was popping up in small towns and hamlets surrounding the District. In Cumberland County, Maryland, a parade of the local chapter "took place through the streets following an initiation." On a Sunday evening in Hagerstown, Maryland, two Klansmen entered the United Brethren Church "and presented the pastor a money contribution." Somehow, Davidson learned of the chapters' plans to march through the city from start to finish. He requested a meeting with Sullivan and was blunt. There would be a race riot if they were granted a permit to march. As they had done during Red Summer, Black Washingtonians would defend their families and communities by any means and never yield to any intimidation. Did Sullivan really want a repeat of 1919?[135]

He did not. In a move that culminated two years of progress for the branch, Sullivan told Davidson there would be no parade. Francis Stephens, of the city's corporation counsel, issued an order: "Processions and parades, except funerals, shall not be allowed except by permit of the major and superintendent of the police." The regulation added a provision that targeted the KKK specifically: "No permit…for any procession or parade of any group, body, or organization [in which] members…are so costumed, dressed, masked or disguised as to be unrecognizable." Johnson offered Davidson hearty congratulations for not only the Klan's defeat but also the positive coverage that had come with it: "I must compliment you not only on the work you did regarding the Ku Klux Klan in Washington, but on the very effective publicity you secured on the matter."[136]

The Branch's Anti-Lynching Campaign

The branch's new agenda of activism also included the barbarism of lynching. The national office created an anti-lynching committee in July 1916 in the wake of a brutal episode of mob violence in Waco, Texas. Two months before, Jesse Washington, an eighteen-year-old farmhand, was lynched before a crowd of fifteen thousand. He had allegedly murdered Lucy Frye, the wife of his white employer, after a trivial argument over

The charred corpse of Jesse Washington, lynched in Waco, Texas, in May 1916. The branch formed an anti-lynching committee two years after this brutal killing. *Library of Congress (LC-USZ62-38917).*

the proper care of the couple's mules. W.E.B. Du Bois provided extensive coverage of the "Waco Horror" in the July issue of *The Crisis* for its gory details and the rare use of photography that captured unmasked participants (including one man who applauds the violence) shamelessly making no attempts to conceal their identities.[137]

Women were victims of vigilante justice as well. Such was the case with Mary Turner in Brooks County, Georgia, in May 1918. Though she was eight months pregnant, seventeen men seized her when she publicly threatened to press charges against the mob who murdered her husband, Hayes, one of eleven men implicated in an alleged murder conspiracy against Hampton Smith, a white plantation owner. The young mother was hanged by her ankles and set ablaze. Her abdomen was split open; the fetus fell to the ground, gave "two feeble cries," only then "to be crushed by the heel of one of the white men present." The mob then "riddled [Turner] with bullets." The *Associated Press* justified the violence by saying "the people in their indignant mood took exception to her remarks as well as her attitude." Another newspaper editorialized that Turner, a "she bear," deserved her lynching because "she flew into such a rage and uttered such vile curses upon the women of Brooks County."[138]

The branch created its own anti-lynching committee after the Turner killing. Jesse Washington, Mary Turner and others were on the minds of members as they listened to Congressman Leonidas Dyer speak at their mass meeting at the Howard Theater on April 17, 1921. Davidson arranged the invitation. A progressive Missouri Republican, Dyer represented the majority-Black Twelfth Congressional District that encompassed the St. Louis area. Competition for jobs between Black southerners who settled in the area during the Great Migration and immigrants from Europe resulted in a race riot in July 1917 that left two white police officers and thirty-five Black residents dead. Dyer initiated an investigation into the riot. The branch, represented by Nannie Helen Burroughs, weighed in on the inquiry as well. As both a member and the superintendent of the National Association for Colored Women's Department for the Suppression of Lynching and Mob Violence, she testified to the House Rules Committee on the lawlessness against Black people that pervaded the South and criticized how precipitators of mob violence would "embolden the lawless element of the country." Burroughs concluded with an impassioned plea: "I come this morning to ask you, in behalf of my people, what are you going to do about this matter?"[139]

Burroughs's testimony strengthened Dyer's conclusions that government

U.S. Representative Leonidas Dyer of Missouri spoke often at branch mass meetings to garner support for federal anti-lynching bills he introduced in the late 1910s and 1920s. *Library of Congress (LC-DIG-npcc-21517).*

Activist, educator and orator Nannie Helen Burroughs. *Library of Congress (LC-USZ62-79903).*

intervention was necessary. On April 1, 1918, he introduced a bill to make lynching a federal crime. In his floor speech, Dyer stated that lynching warranted as much attention as child labor and Prohibition: "Are the rights of property, or what a citizen shall drink, or the ages and conditions under which children shall work, any more important to the Nation than life itself?" The bill was one of the many numerous anti-lynching measures introduced, but it received the most testimonial support from the NAACP. Neval Thomas represented both the national office and the branch in hearings. Dyer had spoken at the Howard Theater meeting to garner support for a revised version of his 1918 bill. On January 26, 1922, it passed on a 231–119 vote in the House. The Senate scheduled committee hearings and floor debate for June. There was hope for its passage and signature by President Harding. To branch officials and members, the District seemed to be making progress on racial justice.[140]

JIM CROW AT THE LINCOLN MEMORIAL DEDICATION

The Lincoln Memorial dedication ceremony on May 30, 1922, instead provided a rude awakening. On that muggy Memorial Day, Whitefield McKinlay was steaming hot, but the climate had nothing to do with it. A businessman and real estate agent, McKinlay had served under President William Howard Taft as the first Black collector of customs at Georgetown. He now headed the branch's Committee on Police and Firemen, where his job was to increase the number of African Americans on those two forces. The McKinlays expected their green tickets to "Platform Section Five" to provide close proximity to Taft (now chief justice of the Supreme Court), President Warren Harding and Robert Russa Moton, principal of Tuskegee Institute and the keynote dedication speaker. Comfortable wooden chairs would provide pleasant views of the imposing, marble-sculpted "Great Emancipator," the Reflecting Pool filled with water for the first time and the spirit of healing represented by frail Confederate veterans in gray and former soldiers in Union blue gathered together under an American flag.[141]

Instead, the couple was marched by their military escort almost a block's length away from the speakers' platform to a segregated area where Black attendees found hard, backless benches surrounded by overgrown grass and weeds. Only a few chairs dotted the aisles. McKinlay was not happy, and when the marine on duty told him to sit down, he told him he would think about

Right: Whitefield McKinlay, chair of the branch's Committee on Police and Firemen, left the Lincoln Memorial dedication ceremony with thirty other African Americans in protest of the segregated seating arrangements. *Library of Congress (LC-DIG-ggbain-05208)*.

Below: Only African American and white members of the Grand Army of the Republic were permitted to sit together at the ceremony. *Library of Congress (LC-DIG-npcc-06385)*.

Lieutenant Clarence Sherrill, a military aide to President Warren Harding, was responsible for the ceremony's logistics, including the segregated seating arrangements. The branch led an unsuccessful campaign to oust him. *Library of Congress (LC-DIG-npcc-03778).*

it. "Well you better think damned quick," the officer spat. His commanding officer came over to quell the dispute after the marine's swearing resulted in the crowd's request for his removal, but he worsened the situation when he offered a most vile defense for the marine's actions: "That's the only way you can handle these damned niggers."[142]

This nearly resulted in a brawl. Angered at being "Jim Crowed," the McKinlays and thirty others left the ceremony. Very few remained. Black Washingtonians complained to the branch. Its leaders placed blame on Lieutenant Colonel Clarence Sherrill, a native North Carolinian and the commission's executive officer, who had been charged with all the ceremony's logistics, including seating arrangements. The humiliation, coupled with the marine's actions—especially in the presence of women, as one angry letter noted—led to the branch's adoption of a resolution critical of this "most shocking and atrocious treatment." An unsuccessful campaign to oust Sherrill followed. Militants like James Cobb were dismayed, believing that Davidson could have utilized his position to move more aggressively against the colonel.[143]

Neval Thomas was disappointed too. Although he did not criticize Davidson directly, he applauded Cobb and others for challenging the executive secretary's cowardice. Thomas instead rejected Moton's speech. In an October 1923 article published in *The Messenger*, a pro–"New Negro" periodical, he wrote about how those gathered in the "assembled House and Senate" to hear abolitionist Henry Highland Garnet speak about Lincoln in 1865 did so "in deep admiration to his eloquent and scholarly sermon of the Thirteenth Amendment and the meaning of slavery and freedom." In comparison, the "time-serving Moton," Thomas said, did not come close to Garnet's style and substance. The essay marked the beginning of Thomas's path to leading the branch and his desire to mold it into a militant entity.[144]

THE 1922 ANTI-LYNCHING "SILENT PARADE"

Davidson's conservative approach to ousting Sherill stemmed from strategic caution. The colonel was a key figure in the Harding administration, and he did not want to antagonize the president, whose support for the Dyer bill was critical. With the Senate now set to begin debate, how would victory be achieved there? Lawmakers needed to see the legislation's importance through the eyes of the District's Black citizens. Johnson suggested a "silent parade in the city" to several Black women activists. It was not unprecedented; Johnson had organized a similar march in New York City after the 1917 East St. Louis riot. Davidson sought to alleviate dismay over the Sherrill controversy by voicing support for the march, but the logistics and planning tasks fell to the women of the branch, including Mary Church Terrell, Burroughs, Carrie Clifford, Angelina Grimké and future president Emma Frances Grayson Merritt, who organized it as members of the "Committee of One Hundred."[145]

The committee settled on a date that symbolized freedom: June 14, Flag Day. From May to June, the branch initiated a dual campaign to increase membership and bolster support for the march. Davidson arranged for Du Bois to speak at Ebenezer AME Church, John Wesley AME Church and Mount Zion AME Church in a three-day visit to the city the first week in May. In conjunction with the Bethel Literary and Historical Association, the branch held a mass meeting at Metropolitan AME Church the night before the parade. It was difficult for anyone to resist attending. Adorned with

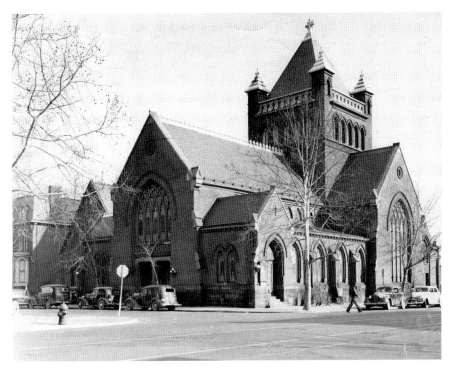

The branch initiated membership campaigns to bolster support for the Anti-Lynching "Silent Parade" at several churches, including John Wesley AME Church. *DC Public Library.*

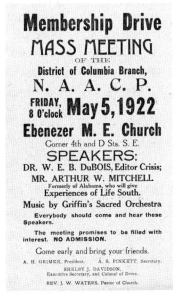

In a three-day visit to Washington in May 1922, W.E.B. Du Bois spoke at several branch mass meetings to garner support for the Silent Parade. *Moorland-Spingarn Research Center, Howard University.*

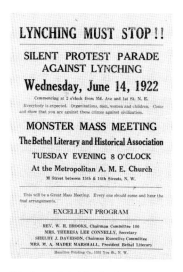

LYNCHING MUST STOP!!

SILENT PROTEST PARADE
AGAINST LYNCHING

Wednesday, June 14, 1922

Commencing at 2 o'clock from Md. Ave and 1st St. N. E.
Everybody is expected. Organizations, men, women and children. Come
and show that you are against these crimes against civilization.

MONSTER MASS MEETING

The Bethel Literary and Historical Association

TUESDAY EVENING 8 O'CLOCK

At the Metropolitan A. M. E. Church

M Street between 15th & 16th Streets, N. W.

This will be a Great Mass Meeting. Every one should come and hear the
final arrangements.

EXCELLENT PROGRAM

REV. W. H. BROOKS, Chairman Committee 100
MRS. THERESA LEE CONNELLY, Secretary
SHELBY J. DAVIDSON, Chairman Executive Committee
MRS. M. A. MADRE MARSHALL, President Bethel Literary

Hamilton Printing Co., 1335 You St., N. W.

The branch held a final mass meeting at Metropolitan AME Church the night before the Silent Parade. *Moorland-Spingarn Research Center, Howard University.*

"LYNCHING MUST STOP!!" at the top, flyers promised, "This will be a Great Mass Meeting" and were direct with its purpose: "Come and show that you are against these crimes of civilization."[146]

The next day "from 2 o'clock until 4 o'clock, the hour for moving, the point of mobilizing at Maryland Ave and First Sts N.E. was a scene of interest" as five thousand Black Washingtonians marched against the inhumanity of lynching. They circled around the Capitol and passed the House and Senate Office Buildings. The timing was no coincidence; the planners made sure that workers leaving their government offices for the day would see them. Children of all ages marched too, reminding observers that they were at risk of a lynch mob just as much as adult men and women. Jesse Washington was a tragic example. Despite the slight inaccuracy about his age, his death was alluded to on one child's sign: "We Are Fifteen Years Old: One of Our Age Was Roasted Alive." Women's signs relayed their place in society as mothers and the loss of their sons and daughters. Several evoked Mary Turner and her unborn child: "We Protest the Burning of Babies and Women...American Cannibalism." Some drew attention to the bill's opponents who were more concerned with its constitutionality than the actions of murderous posses: "Congress Discusses Constitutionality While the Smoke of Burning Bodies Darkens the Heavens." Black veterans closed the parade, their placement a testimonial for their military service to protect democracy.[147]

THE "MAMMY MONUMENT"

The Dyer bill was met with resistance from southern Democratic senators who continuously filibustered it. By December 1922, even liberal Senate Republicans had abandoned efforts to pass it, and no anti-lynching legislation became law for the remainder of the decade. By that time, a new conflict that enabled Thomas to secure the branch presidency

In 1923, Mississippi senator John Sharp Williams introduced a bill to erect "a monument or memory of the faithful mammies of the South" in Washington. *Library of Congress (LC-USZ62-39622).*

surfaced. Shortly after the dedication of Frederick Douglass's home in Anacostia, Mississippi senator John Sharp Williams introduced a proposal "for the erection as a gift to the people of the United States…in the city of Washington, DC…a monument or memory of the faithful mammies of the South." The Committee on the Library took up the bill. Williams's proposal culminated from a post–World War I wave of extolment for the virtues of antebellum southern society from Confederate heritage organizations whose founding principles were rooted in the Lost Cause. These groups included the United Daughters of the Confederacy.[148]

The UDC's Washington chapter felt compelled to create a public representation of faithful slavery. The Great Migration, they believed, was not attributed to harsh economic conditions or white supremacy but the failure of African Americans to understand their "place" and remain there. Black people's troublesome fomentation against the social order was why lynchings occurred. The mammy illustrated the "proper" way for African Americans to behave and maintain peace and affection between the races.[149]

With the District chapter's endorsement, the Jefferson Davis Chapter No. 1650 in Richmond, Virginia, requested that Williams advance the mammy bill. It was the last piece of legislation the retiring senator hoped to pass after a thirty-year career. The *Washington Evening Star* lent immediate and enthusiastic support, arguing that the country had too few monuments dedicated to servants, all the more reason to build one for mammies who "were far more than just servants." They were "guides, counselors and friends to their white, loving families." In late January 1923, the *Star* predicted the monument "would be received with pleasure by a great number of men and women," and "was worthy of being symbolized in stone and bronze."[150]

Black Washingtonians responded with varying solutions. The Northeast Boundary Citizens Association took up a resolution at their Burrsville School meeting against the proposal, viewing it as the ugliest symbol of propaganda against Black women since the Civil War and Reconstruction. However, the association also included a recommendation that if a monument was constructed, it belonged in the South "nearer to the original homes of the 'mammies.'" Comparably, the Civic Center Association argued there should be no monument in the District or anywhere. In a joint statement published in the *Washington Tribune*, President W.D. Nixon and Secretary H.E. Barnett condemned the proposal as the Confederate woman's expression of love for the mammy "in a most despicable way." And what irony it was that these Black women had nursed generations of men who had ushered in the lynching of "over three thousand five hundred men and women in the last thirty-five years."[151]

Thomas placed opposition to the monument in a more personal context. In an open letter to the UDC, Senate leaders and the *New York World* published in the *Star*, he wrote tenderly of his enslaved mother and what she wanted most for her children in a nation she hoped would someday destroy involuntary servitude. "I know the heart of a slave mother [and] its intense longing for better things for her children," he wrote. Her descendants were not entitled to a monument but instead opportunities for "reading the best literature…taking honors at the best universities in the land, and reigning over cultured homes." Democracy, he concluded, was the monument that should be built to the "colored mammy," not a "proposed marble shaft."[152]

Neither the national office nor the branch's official positions were aligned with Thomas. Davidson informed Johnson that "we are standing still with reference to any immediate protest because our organization having been styled by some of the enemies as 'high-browed' this might give opportunity to prove to illiterate Negroes in the South and nearby that our antagonism was directed against them as a class because of the difference in our status."[153]

With the pointed references to illiteracy and class differences, Davidson shared the same Black Washington elite prejudices toward southerners and poor and working-class migrants to the city that he identified as criticisms of the NAACP. He also implied that these groups were incapable of comprehending the monument was an insult to them. He asked Johnson what the best approach was, but the secretary's reply was equally disappointing: "I do not think we can prohibit the erection of the monument." Johnson was not opposed to the memorial; his problem was to have a structure in the capital while white people also "Jim Crow, disenfranchise, and lynch her sons." He instructed Davidson to use "extracts" from Thomas's letter as the organization's official response.[154]

The branch's conservative position was awkward for its female members. Terrell published a scathing letter in the *Star* several days after Thomas's

NAACP executive secretary James Weldon Johnson took a conservative approach on the "Mammy Monument," arguing it should not be built in the District, but in the South. *Library of Congress (LC-USZ62-42992).*

article. Speaking of the pain and anger the statue aroused, she appealed to both races in her condemnation: "It is difficult to see how any women whether white or black, could take any pleasure in a marble statue to perpetuate her memory." She concluded with a prayer for its destruction at the hands of a lightning strike "on a stormy night." It was the only remedy to prevent the mammy's ancestors from being reminded "of the anguish of heart and the physical suffering which the mothers and grandmothers of the race endured for nearly 300 years." Terrell's use of her NACW affiliation—and not a founding member or former vice president of the branch—in her signature was a rebuke of both its neutral stance on the monument and the gross misjudgment of its conservative, all-male leadership that they were standing up for Black women by defending it.[155]

In February 1923, the bill passed successfully in the Senate on a voice vote with seventy-five members present. It was now up to the House of Representatives' Committee on the Library to schedule a final vote and

Sculptor Ulric Stonewall Jackson Dunbar with a model of his proposed "Mammy" statue. *Library of Congress (LC-DIG-npcc-24343).*

officially enact the bill. The UDC began accepting design proposals from D.C. sculptors who wanted the honor of designing a local and national attraction. The *Star* and *Washington Post* stirred interest and excitement by reporting the call for submissions as a competition for the best design. Three artists emerged as leading contenders: Ulric Stonewall Jackson Dunbar, "one of the most widely known sculptors in the National Capital"; George Julian Zolnay, a Hungarian immigrant and former president of the Arts

George Julian Zolnay, former president of the Arts Club of Washington and the "Sculptor of the Confederacy." *Library of Congress (LC-DIG-npcc-08432).*

Club of Washington whose creations of Jefferson Davis across the South earned him the sobriquet "Sculptor of the Confederacy"; and Ethel Leach Carpenter, a socialite and former student at the George Washington University and the Corcoran Gallery of Art.[156]

The branch's silence and Terrell's letter galvanized Black women to protest the monument. Several branch women, including Terrell and Merritt, joined the Phyllis Wheatley YWCA in a grassroots campaign to defeat it. They solicited the support of churches, civic associations, business leaders and newspaper editors and marched to Capitol Hill to deliver petitions to Vice President Calvin Coolidge and House Speaker Frederick Gillett. The coalition had adopted a diplomatic approach, but not everyone preferred that method. While Terrell had hoped for the monument's destruction by an act of nature, the *Eagle* threatened man-made demolition. "We will put a bomb under it," the publication ominously promised the UDC if the statue was completed "in the defiance of our wishes."[157]

By the summer, the anti-monument forces prevailed. Frederic Haskin, who published a weekly *Star* "Answers to Questions" column, closed the subject when a curious reader inquired about the statue. Amid a variety of questions about scallions, Charles Dickens's home, D.C. summer temperatures and the size of the German army, Haskin wrote of the mammy memorial's fate: "The bill did not pass the House so it will be necessary to introduce it in another session of Congress before further progress can be made." It never was.[158]

NEVAL THOMAS VERSUS THE DC PUBLIC LIBRARY

In January 1924, Cobb wrote to NAACP Vice President Arthur Spingarn that "at present the branch is in a very bad way." He did not elaborate, but it was a jab at Davidson's leadership as executive secretary. Sherrill had not been terminated, the Dyer anti-lynching bill had been defeated and the branch's position on the mammy monument stung. Davidson did not espouse the radicalism necessary for change that Cobb, Carter G. Woodson and others sought after Red Summer. Archibald Grimké was still the branch president, but now at the age of seventy-five, he was rumored to be considering resignation. Cobb feared it was true. Grimké was held in high regard by "the people of Washington of all classes and all colors," Cobb wrote to Spingarn. His inquiry was just as much about his personal admiration for him as it was for his desire for Grimké to reclaim leadership from Davidson.[159]

Spingarn assured Cobb that the rumors were false, and Grimké remained in office for the remainder of the year. However, in January 1925, Grimké chose not to seek reelection, and Thomas was unanimously elected the branch's second president. His first battle as its leader began three years before and was an example of how he wished to push the organization in a more confrontational and militant direction. An October 1922 *Washington Times* editorial, "Value of Public Library," reminded residents they were privileged to be served by a world-class system: "Its service to all classes and all ages is tireless, efficient, and tactful." The city's "Congressional Library," museums and art galleries hardly offered the same "homelike atmosphere… that one finds in the strictly local institution. The public library is for the home people of the District of Columbia."[160]

In 1905, two years after its opening, a training course for women aged eighteen to thirty-five "to prepare [them] for junior positions" was established by city librarian George Bowerman and directed by librarian Clara Herbert. The class did not automatically guarantee employment with the system, but applicants were drawn to the high percentage of vacancies in the junior staff that "are ordinarily filled by graduates of the training class."[161]

For Thomas, there was just one problem. African American female applicants were not considered, and as he wrote in response to the *Herald* article, there were also no people of color working at the library: "Every employee there, from the librarian himself down to the janitor and watchman, is white." As taxpayers, he argued, Black Washingtonians were just as entitled to equal hiring opportunities offered by the class.[162]

Bowerman disputed Thomas's employment discrimination charges. "Why, all my charwomen are colored," he stated, according to the *Washington Eagle*. However, the city librarian did state his intention "to continue his policy of only allowing white girls to enter the professional service and the

Above: The Central Public Library in Mount Vernon Square. *DC Public Library.*

Left: George F. Bowerman, DC chief librarian from 1904 to 1940, did not permit female African American students to enroll in library training courses and hired no Black librarians during his tenure. *DC Public Library.*

training class." Bowerman had reached that decision in 1917. Keeping in line with the city's segregated school system, he made recommendations "for the establishment of public library branches in colored school buildings." These facilities, he reported, "would naturally be conducted by colored librarians who, of course, should be trained." Acknowledging that there was "no library school for training colored librarians other than the Howard University Library," Bowerman concluded that "it would not be practicable to train such colored librarians in the library's own training class." Thomas reminded him that the Library of Congress (where he once worked) and other federal and municipal workplaces were "far ahead of him in enlightened policy" and that even some of the most conservative members of Congress from the South "secure clerical positions for colored men and women."[163]

As branch president, Thomas believed he could draw attention to the class and hiring discrimination when he revisited the issue in February 1925 with a published letter to Bowerman. However, the library chief did not relent, and Thomas was unable to harness enthusiasm from the membership for an aggressive response. Grimké and Davidson never regarded the issue as a priority since the library's 1903 opening included a policy of integration. Black patrons were never denied access to books, space and services in the grandiose Mount Vernon Square building, but that was lost on the branch's elite members. The controversy was an example of their acceptance of the white status quo and unwillingness to challenge it. The library was an integrated space, and that was sufficient. Ultimately, Thomas's attacks were regarded as more of a personal dispute with Bowerman than a legitimate issue.[164]

Lack of coverage by the District's press (Black and white) further deprived Thomas of the opportunity to garner outrage from Black Washingtonians. Only the *Baltimore Afro-American* and the *New York Amsterdam News* published Thomas's letter, and it was just a one-day story. Efforts to implement equal library employment opportunities remained a long struggle. It was not until 1943 that the first African American librarian, Althea Howard, was hired by the system.[165]

The 1925 and the 1926 Ku Klux Klan Parades

By June, the library controversy had become a distant memory. Something eerie occurred at Howard University. A student received a Ku Klux Klan circular the previous month. As there was no African American president of the historically Black institution (Mordecai Johnson would become the first in 1926), the alarmed student complained to Kelly Miller, one of the most influential Black faculty members on campus. Who had sent it? Was the Klan planning something sinister against students? Miller suspected it was connected to the proposed Klan parade in Washington in August. He sent copies of the handbill to Postmaster General Harry S. New and the District commissioners and notified Thomas and the national office. "I am sure you want to be fully informed as to every aspect of this situation," he wrote to James Weldon Johnson. "The NAACP is…best calculated to render this service."[166]

Miller did not receive a reply from New, but Daniel Garges, secretary of the board of commissioners, notified him the matter was referred to the city's Detective Bureau. He informed Miller that "Detective-Sergeants Jones and Jackson canvassed the various printers of this city and failed to find that the attached handbill was printed by any of them." The pair also noted that "colored business people living and doing business in the 8th District" also

The Ku Klux Klan marches down Pennsylvania Avenue on August 8, 1925. *DC Public Library, Star Collection © Washington Post.*

received the handbills and concluded "they were mailed on a railroad train somewhere in the State of Pennsylvania."[167]

Miller's hunch that the circular was related to the parade was correct. In 1922, Davidson had prevented a local contingent of Klansmen from marching in Washington with the support of law enforcement. This time, Thomas faced insurmountable challenges. The Klan boasted almost four million members by 1925, which guaranteed a larger demonstration. A more sympathetic police department, led by Assistant Superintendent Charles Evans, granted the organization a permit to march as long as the robed participants remained unmasked.[168]

Thomas galvanized branch opposition to the parade with a "Don't Let the Ku Klux Catch You Napping" membership campaign. The Klan responded with an ominous message. A telegram, addressed to attorney and branch official Edward P. Lovett, threatened trouble for African Americans in the District (and from everywhere else) "after July 4, 1925." Signed by

Dr. H.W. Evans, KKK imperial wizard, leads members down Pennsylvania Avenue in September 1926. The parade was smaller than the previous year. *Library of Congress (LC-DIG-ds-12592).*

"Kommittee," it warned: "All Negroes entering into or remaining in the District of Columbia, will do so at their own risk."[169]

Undaunted, the branch continued with its opposition campaign. However, despite protests to President Calvin Coolidge and the District commissioners, the Klan marched down Pennsylvania Avenue on a hot August 8. Messages focused on the fears of immigration and a non-Protestant culture and the bogeyman of Catholicism: "Americans be on guard," read one distributed circular. The racial rhetoric was ugly but somewhat more restrained. H.A. Culledge, an Ohio pastor, said, "The glory of the black man is his black skin and the glory of the white man is his white skin. As long as the black remain black and the white remain white, all is well."[170]

The *Post*, estimating the crowd at 30,000–35,000, described the event as "one of the greatest demonstrations this city has ever known." The *Star* placed attendance much higher at 100,000 and was equally positive. The "vivid demonstration," "spectacular feature" and "colorful march" descriptions depicted the parade as an enjoyable circus or carnival. The *Afro-American*, by contrast, described an unimpressive spectacle that proved Washingtonians did not want the "Kluxeties" in their city at all. "Enthusiasm among spectators was apparently lacking and there was little applause as the monotonous figures in white went by." Thomas worked with several Catholic and Jewish organizations to prevent a second (but smaller) Klan parade in Washington in September 1926 but was unsuccessful.[171]

Legacy of Neval Thomas

Thomas's zeal to radically make justice out of all injustices marked his tenure as the 1920s came to a close. For all his defeats with the library and the Klan parade, Thomas celebrated significant victories. Wilson was now deceased and buried in the National Cathedral, but his Democratic allies in Congress repeatedly reintroduced the same anti-intermarriage and segregated streetcar bills that Grimké had fought. Under his leadership, the branch prevented all of them from becoming law. In 1926, an aggressive campaign to abolish the capital's segregated bathing beaches successfully came to a close when Thomas demanded House Appropriations Committee chairman Thomas Madden eliminated allocate funding for them. Later that year, Thomas led a delegation of concerned citizens to the Interior Department to investigate reports of segregation in several departments. Secretary Hubert Work relented "in an unprecedented backdown," as

Children playing at the Tidal Basin whites-only bathing beach in 1925. Pressure from the branch to build a beach for African Americans led the Senate to defund both sites. *Library of Congress (LC-DIG-hec-30164).*

Thomas called it, and issued a memorandum ending separate working conditions in the Pensions Bureau, where most African Americans worked. The branch had wrestled with the District commissioners for eleven years, but Thomas was its first leader to urge an American president to appoint a Black man as one of those three officials when he wrote to Coolidge in 1927. He irritated the Office of the Architect of the Capitol with published calls to remove monuments of Confederate leaders Robert E. Lee and Alexander H. Stephens from National Statuary Hall in the U.S. Capitol.[172]

Many Washingtonians praised Thomas's militancy. Miller once opined in his regular *Afro-American* "Kelly Miller Says" column that the branch president "has well-earned the sobriquet the John Brown of the District of Columbia." "Neval Thomas…is carrying on with like devotion and marvelous coverage," another *Afro* editorial said. "It is nothing less than marvelous when a Negro leader, anywhere in the United States, has the courage to fight the battles of his race as Thomas has done."[173]

For all the accolades, Thomas's character prevented him from securing more victories as a champion of the rights of Black Washingtonians. His brashness alienated many allies. As a member of the national NAACP

Board of Directors, he feuded with Du Bois, accusing him of providing tepid coverage of the branch's anti-segregation work in *The Crisis*. He also made allegations that Du Bois awarded himself the Spingarn Medal. Thomas also targeted Johnson, charging that he evaded segregation issues as much as possible. Even some branch members faced his wrath for any perceived passivity in fighting inequality. In January 1928, Lafayette Hershaw, Thomas's key ally in the removal of John Milton Waldron, opposed the branch's Interior Department desegregation campaign. As a Land Office investigator, Hershaw bizarrely claimed that he and all the clerks were "satisfied with the [Jim Crow] conditions." Outraged, Thomas swiftly pressured the executive committee to demand Hershaw's resignation. He complied and soon withdrew from all branch activities.[174]

By April 1929, Thomas's crusade against racism had taken its toll on his physical health. The fifty-six-year-old bachelor took a break and traveled to France, Italy and Switzerland. He returned in December, then journeyed to the South for the warm, soothing bathhouses in Hot Springs, Arkansas. He needed the rest. The branch had much work to do in the coming decade. Not only did Thomas wanted to continue the fight, but he also believed he had a moral obligation to do so. Sadly though, it would not be his fate.[175]

5

"MAKE PENNSYLVANIA AVENUE TREMBLE!"

On April 15, 1930, at 4:00 p.m., Black Washingtonians gathered in Howard University's Andrew Rankin Memorial Chapel to bid farewell to their "militant Negro champion," Neval Thomas. He had succumbed two days before at 1122 Fairmont Street NW, the home of his sister, Sue Williston. Thomas's condition turned worse upon his return from Arkansas, and he suffered a paralyzing stroke three weeks before his death.[176]

Many paid tribute. Robert W. Brooks, pastor of Lincoln Memorial Congregational Church, of which Thomas had been a member and trustee, and Mordecai Johnson, the first Black president of Howard University, conducted the services. Several branch officers and members served as pallbearers: Garnet Wilkinson, Archibald S. Pinkett and John C. Bruce. James Cobb, Nannie Helen Burroughs, George William Cook and Charles Edward Russell attended the service as representatives of the national office. The branch later organized a memorial tribute at Lincoln in October 1930 for Thomas and Grimké, who died in February. Kelly Miller, who worked with and admired both men deeply, eulogized Grimké. It was befitting that one of the most prominent individuals in the city's school system would pay homage to Thomas as a fellow educator. That honor went to Roscoe Conkling Bruce.[177]

BRANCH ELECTS EMMA MERRITT

Always "an outstanding champion" for the NAACP, Thomas's will included $500 for the association, which Sue sent to New York as executor of her brother's estate. At a special meeting on May 28, 1930, the branch's executive committee further honored Thomas by unanimously electing Emma Frances Grayson Merritt, supervising principal of the "colored" schools' Eleventh Division, to complete his unexpired presidential term. Born in January 1860 in Dumfries, Virginia, Merritt moved to Washington with her family at the age of three. She graduated from the "M Street" High School (later Dunbar High School) in 1875 and pursued undergraduate and graduate studies at Howard University and the Columbian College (now George Washington University), respectively. In that same year, Merritt began her career as a primary grade teacher at the Stevens School. She became principal of the Garnet School in 1895 and director of primary instruction in 1897. Merritt also established the first kindergarten for Black children.[178]

Merritt's work garnered attention and praise from prominent District officials and citizens and also opened opportunities on many school issues. Frank W. Ballou, the superintendent of schools, asked the Board of Education to establish two "laboratory" schools to implement Merritt's reformist teaching methodologies and remarked on her contributions to advancement in education: "Miss Merritt has blazed a new trail in modern education." In January 1907, the Woman's Convention Auxiliary to the National Baptist Convention gathered at the Nineteenth Street Baptist Church to address plans "to erect a well-equipped building in the District of Columbia in which all the arts and professions in which women engage will be taught in practical and comprehensive courses." Merritt was one of five "special guests" at the convention to advise the project. In a tribute to her work and reputation for securing teaching positions for Black youth throughout the country, but particularly in the South, Carter G. Woodson noted "that the District of Columbia has never had a teacher whose influence has been more widely exerted for the enlightenment of the Negroes at large." Board of Education meetings often included testimonials from parents and officials about Merritt's "remarkable educational record." She was eligible for retirement at the age of seventy in January 1930 but not yet ready to leave her beloved profession. Nor was the board; her contract was extended to June 30. The committee's decision to elect Merritt to the presidency also had much to do with her civic work.

She led the Teachers' Benefit and Annuity Association for many years, served on the board of the Southwest Settlement House and chaired the Committee on Finance of the Phyllis Wheatley YWCA.[179]

Merritt began her presidency tackling issues in local law enforcement and national criminal justice, focusing first on Black police officers in the District. She theorized that more African Americans on the city's police force meant more of a Black presence in neighborhoods, which would help end shootings by white policemen. A branch investigation revealed that a fair representation of Black officers in the Metropolitan Police Department numbered at 250. However, there were only 45 due to retirements with no new appointments. A joint statement from Herbert Crosby, secretary of the Civil Service Commission, and Detective Bureau Inspector Shelby that "colored men do not take the examinations," did not appease Merritt, who interviewed the three officials along with E.W. Baker of the *Baltimore Afro-American* in August 1930. After probing deeper, Merritt discovered cases of young Black men not applying because "there are no inducements." The branch initiated a data collection project study to determine the reason for the examination failures and, as the *Afro* reported, "induce others to become candidates in order to offset the claims of the officials."[180]

Although police brutality in the city would not draw the attention of the branch and the full force of its legal staff for several more years, allies suggested its leaders extend the fight beyond the employment of Black officers. "The methods do not produce results," Dan O'Brien of the American Brotherhood and Welfare Association told the branch at a meeting at the Phyllis Wheatley YWCA Building in June 1930, after initiating an investigation of mistreatment of four Black prisoners at the Sixth Precinct. "We are held up as a mirror of disgrace. We can put a stop to these impositions, but we will have to take action. We will have to organize."[181]

Virginia McGuire Becomes Branch President

After Merritt's death in June 1933, interim branch president Virginia "Jennie" Richardson McGuire took action by aggressively pursuing justice against police brutality, especially for Black women. McGuire, a truant officer, came from a prominent Washington family. Her mother, Ida Richardson, "was one of the first Negro teachers" in the city, and her father, George H. Richardson, was a physician, attorney and the first president of the Black Federation of Civic Associations. Her husband, Robert, a pharmacist, established the McGuire Funeral Home at 1820 Ninth Street NW, which he and Jennie operated as co-proprietors.[182]

The branch's protests against the Metropolitan Police Department (which dated to the 1919 Red Summer riot) continued in the 1930s as African Americans, particularly women, faced abuse at the hands of white police officers. In December 1932, two Black women, Virgie Togood and her sister-in-law Mattie Ford, were walking in Southeast Washington when two officers pulled up alongside them in their cruiser and catcalled, "Hello babies, hello sweethearts," to them. Ford was slapped when she protested the vulgarities. George W. Beasley, president of the Federation of Civic Associations, a network of African American organizations and a pharmacist, who was closing his store with two colleagues

Virginia McGuire, the branch's second female president (and last until the 1970s), steered the organization in a progressive direction in the fight against lynching and police brutality. *DC History Center.*

and witnessed the confrontation, intervened by telling the officers, "Don't do that." Outraged, they ordered Wesley and his companions to line up against a fence, where one drew his gun and threatened to "blow their brains out." The *Afro* ran an article, "DC Cops Terror to Women." The coverage and Wesley's position with the federation were enough to secure a Police Court hearing but nothing more; the officers were exonerated and faced no disciplinary action.[183]

One of the most violent cases McGuire investigated involved Cornelia Diggs, aged sixty, and her daughter, Dedia Coates, who were attacked by officers W.W. Humphreys and Henry Mazurski in the early morning hours of November 8, 1933, at their home in Anacostia. Without identifying themselves first, the pair forced their way in by breaking down two doors, but not before firing multiple bullets into the house that struck a kitchen buffet and the staircase. Interviewed by an *Afro* investigator, Diggs stated that the "policemen were intoxicated" and proceeded to drag her by her hair from the bedroom to the first floor, where she and Coates, still in their nightclothes, were beaten before being arrested and charged with disorderly conduct at the Eleventh Precinct station. The *Afro* reported that Humphreys and Mazurski had inflicted much damage on Diggs: "two blackened eyes, a badly battered face and bruises about the shoulders and left leg."[184]

On behalf of Black Washingtonians who were aware of the beatings Diggs and Coates suffered, McGuire and other allies sought justice in both cases. She collaborated with the Hillsdale Civic Association in Anacostia to get both women acquitted of their alleged crimes in a Police Court hearing. The officers were never charged, but the outcomes for Diggs and Coates, albeit rare, were legal victories nevertheless.[185]

The Second Anti-Lynching Fight

McGuire also displayed this progressive leadership during the federal anti-lynching campaign in Washington. For the branch, advocacy work in this area was just as important as police brutality in the capital since it was akin to lynching in the South. "Niggers have no constitutional rights," a policeman spat in the 1930s. "The Constitution was made for white men." Lynch mobs believed the same. Eight persons (six Black and two white) died by mob violence in 1932, but the following year saw a dramatic increase in lynchings to twenty-six (twenty-four Black and two white). No lynching ever occurred in the District, but Black Washingtonians were horrified on October 18, 1933, when George Armwood, a twenty-year-old laborer, was brutally murdered at the hands of a mob less than three hours away in Princess Anne, Maryland, on the Eastern Shore. McGuire, Mary Church Terrell and others convened a one-day conference at the Phyllis Wheatley YWCA in early November in which prominent attorneys, activists and journalists urged the need for a concerted effort against mob violence.[186]

The focus of the economic impact from the dire unemployment that was engulfing the country at the NAACP's 1932 annual meeting in Washington forced police brutality and lynching from the agenda. This was another reason the branch advocated strongly for federal anti-lynching legislation. In January 1934, Senate Democrats Edward Costigan of Colorado and Robert Wagner of New York provided hope when they jointly introduced a bill (S. 1878) that was sponsored by the NAACP. The branch was heartened; many members recalled their participation in the 1922 parade to generate anti-lynching support. Although it did not punish lynchers directly, the Costigan-Wagner bill was similar to the Dyer bill in its robustness: (1) a mob was defined

Praising "the fine record of the District of Columbia branch," NAACP executive secretary Walter White supported its request to host the 1932 annual meeting in Washington. *Library of Congress (LC-USF34-013343-C).*

as three or more individuals; (2) federal authorities would intervene if state or local officials did not take prosecutorial action in thirty days; (3) public officials who did not protect a victim or participated in the crime themselves (as often was the case) would be subjected to a fine, imprisonment or both; and (4) a county or multiple jurisdictions where a lynching took place would be levied with a fine. The legislation stalled in the Senate shortly after its introduction by southern Democrats and conservative Republicans from the North and West. However, the branch believed there was another window of opportunity: Franklin Roosevelt, with his New Deal programs and informal "Black Cabinet," was viewed favorably. And First Lady Eleanor Roosevelt was considered a liberal advocate on political and social issues, including racial equality. Both, McGuire mused, were the allies the branch needed.[187]

She was only partially correct. McGuire, who became branch president after a special election in March 1934, wrote to Roosevelt in October upon learning about yet another grisly murder when twenty-three-year-old Claude Neal was castrated, mutilated and repeatedly lowered and raised in hanging in front of a crowd of two thousand for allegedly murdering a nineteen-year-old white woman in Marianna, Florida. The president did not respond. Eleanor Roosevelt, by comparison, had a warm relationship with McGuire and urged the passage of anti-lynching legislation and other civil rights measures as the guest speaker at the branch's mass meetings, often at Metropolitan AME Church.[188]

Power in numbers was an obvious asset, but the branch leadership also believed there was viable strength in voices. In late March, Nannie Burroughs suggested to McGuire the resurrection of a speakers' bureau—the one Archibald Grimké established no longer existed—to communicate the branch's agenda and goals and bolster membership. McGuire endorsed the idea, and the bureau eventually comprised about ten to fifteen oratorical powerhouses, including Terrell and Carter G. Woodson.[189]

Do not look at the Negro.

His earthly problems are ended.

Instead, look at the seven WHITE children who gaze at this gruesome spectacle.

Is it horror or gloating on the face of the neatly dressed seven-year-old girl on the right?

Is the tiny four-year-old on the left old enough, one wonders, to comprehend the barbarism her elders have perpetrated?

Rubin Stacy, the Negro, who was lynched at Fort Lauderdale, Florida, on July 19, 1935, for "threatening and frightening a white woman," suffered PHYSICAL torture for a few short hours. But what psychological havoc is being wrought in the minds of the white children? Into what kinds of citizens

The branch lobbied aggressively for passage of the Senate's Costigan-Wagner anti-lynching bill after the brutal murder of Rubin Stacy in Marianna, Florida, in 1935. *DC History Center.*

CRIME CONFERENCE
AND THE "ROPE PROTESTS," 1934

A final opportunity to get the federal government to place attention on the barbarism of lynching came at the end of the year when the Department of Justice hosted its annual National Crime Conference in Washington. Scheduled for four days beginning on December 10, five hundred judges, police commissioners, sheriffs and prison officials gathered at Memorial Continental Hall, the headquarters of the Daughters of the American Revolution, at 1776 D Street NW to address the causes and prevention of crime, criminal courts and prosecution, parole, probation, pardons and detection and apprehension of crime and criminals. These issues fit the agenda for those who sought to bring an end to lynching, so branch officials and other city activists were bewildered when Attorney General Homer Cummings refused to place it in conference sessions. There was no need, Cummings reasoned in a reply to NAACP attorney Charles Hamilton Houston's telegram about the matter; discussions at each session were open to any topic, including lynching: "There is absolutely no limitation as to topics. At such sessions, particular crimes, including kidnaping and lynchings, will no doubt come in for special consideration." As Cummings reasoned, lynching as a possible, informal discussion subject would suffice.[190]

The branch decided to picket the meeting in protest of the omission. McGuire appealed to District police superintendent Ernest Brown for a permit. He refused, but that did not matter. Undeterred, NAACP assistant secretary Roy Wilkins, District branch attorney Edward P. Lovett, *Baltimore Afro-American* editor George Murphy and attorney Emmett Dorsey stood on the sidewalk outside of the Hall at 12:30 p.m. on the first day of the conference carrying signs that drew attention to the exclusion. McGuire, Pinkett and George E.C. Hayes, director of the branch's legal staff, accompanied them. The group's presence was strategically clever timing, as their demonstration began as attendees strolled out for the lunchtime break. It was impossible not to see the placards. Five minutes into their protest, police captain Edward Kelly confronted the group and demanded their permit. Upon being told they had attempted to obtain one, Kelly ordered them to "go back and see Major Brown and get one." At police headquarters, the Crime Prevention Bureau's Inspector Edwards refused their request, citing Roosevelt's statement on lynching as justification. The reasoning was just as inaccurate as it was bizarre; Roosevelt had not yet addressed the conference, and a presidential statement condemning lynching was irrelevant to its exclusion from the proceedings. At 2:30 p.m., the group returned to the conference and, with no permit, were threatened with arrest if they did not disperse. The men refused and were transported to "No. 3 precinct" where the police blotter charge read "violating the sign law," although according to the *Afro*, the real reason in the eyes of the station officers was the permit.[191]

The president delivered on his promise to mention lynchings when he spoke to the conference that evening. He did not endorse the Costigan-Wagner bill but denounced the murders and acknowledged they were now a national problem: "Lynchings are no longer confined to one section of the country, unfortunately." The branch was pleased that Roosevelt had at least taken that action, but was still determined to respond to the police department's obstruction of the conference protest. A new strategy was needed. On December 13, McGuire gathered fifty-five participants at the Phyllis Wheatley YWCA and instructed them to write messages on signs smaller than the ones the group was arrested for. She also provided each person with a piece of rope twelve inches in length to be worn around

Virginia McGuire (*second from right*) with national NAACP and branch officials outside the National Crime Conference in 1934 to protest the exclusion of lynching from the conference. *Library of Congress (LC-USZ62-33784).*

the neck to evoke a grimmer image of lynching victims. Returned to the conference by Black-owned taxicab companies, the group congregated on the sidewalk in eleven groups of five wearing the ropes and carrying the signs that now fit within the "sign law" guidelines. McGuire designated one leader of each group to be arrested if there was a repeat of police intervention. Like the 1922 Silent Parade, each protester did not speak, and the messages were just as stark. Owing Plummer, a native of North Carolina and student at Howard University, held a sign that simply read "4 Women, 45 Years" in reference to the four Black women who had been lynched in her state from 1885 to 1930, one of whom just for allegedly being economically prosperous. Another read "5504 Lynchings in 80 Years." However, unlike the demonstration twelve years before, the use of the ropes conveyed a more assertive anti-lynching message.[192]

The "Rope Protests" resulted in a victory. Although the attorney general had resisted the inclusion of lynching and efforts to permit NAACP delegates, he invited members of the Washington Bar Association, an African American organization, to attend the conference due to the pressure exerted by the demonstrators. The branch earned national accolades as newspapers favorably reported the activists' tactics as a form of nonviolent "direct action" that achieved more than a series of speeches ever could. One account celebrated how the use of the rope elicited comments from the conference attendees and "drew all newspaper photographers." The *Baltimore Afro-American* hailed the demonstration as "smart and original." The group's teachers, pastors and journalists illustrated McGuire's connections with Washington's academic, religious and media circles. More importantly, the participation of undergraduate students—who ranged from freshmen to seniors and comprised twenty-nine of the fifty-five total—and Bertha Lomack, a printer's assistant was a stellar example of McGuire's ability to organize a coalition that spanned generational and class lines. This was not lost on the branch, which issued a statement after the conference: "No sacrifice is to [*sic*] great to wipe out this barbarity. The young people in Washington have set an example for the rest of the country. No one of us should be too educated or too dignified to fight lynching."[193]

Burroughs articulated that message at a branch mass meeting at Vermont Avenue Baptist Church on December 29, two weeks after the conference protests. Before a packed audience of one thousand members, she spoke directly to the young adults in the pews as though they were her own children: "You, the third generation from slavery, have no right to sit here tonight and enjoy the blessings from the sacrifices of other generations, unless you too, are willing to shoulder the burdens and responsibilities facing your race, and carry on!" Burroughs had been skeptical the Costigan-Wagner bill would pass and urged those gathered to utilize their power to agitate for what was sure to be a long-term battle. "There are enough people to make Pennsylvania Avenue tremble," she declared. She framed the call for Black Washingtonians to demand their rights by challenging them to ponder what was on the minds of both white congressional leaders and white southerners: "Lynchings and burnings start as much in the federal government as in Mississippi. All whites want to know here in Washington or down in Mississippi or Alabama or Tennessee is 'Will they take it? And how much will they take?'." Burroughs's prediction on the legislation was correct. It met a similar fate as the Dyer bill when southern senators repeatedly filibustered it and adjourned on June 20, 1936, without taking any action.[194]

Conservatism Takes Over

In April 1935, one week after inviting Eleanor Roosevelt to speak at a mass meeting at Metropolitan AME Church, McGuire resigned from the branch presidency. Some of the District's Black press reported rumors that her decision was forced in retaliation for disinviting Du Bois, who had resigned from the association in June 1934 in protest over disputes with White and Wilkins. Others believed it was attributed it to her snub of Mordecai Johnson. The Howard University president was fighting harsh accusations from Arthur Mitchell of Illinois, the first African American Democrat elected to Congress, that he was transforming the institution into a bastion of Communist ideology. McGuire refused to corroborate the gossip but said that "a lack of cooperation between the executive committee and other committees, and obstructive limitation upon the right of the president" were the primary factors. Health was cited as a minor reason. McGuire did not mention names, but her remarks were an indictment of Pinkett's leadership as executive secretary. Like Shelby Davidson in the 1920s, he exerted influence in the leadership body. McGuire's resignation came with a price. The Executive Committee elected John C. Bruce, supervising principal of public schools, to succeed her, and with Pinkett, the two men abandoned McGuire's progressivism and steered the organization in a more conservative direction.[195]

The most vivid example was the branch's relationship with the New Negro Alliance (NNA), one of the nation's first grassroots organizations

STAY OUT!!
Peoples Drug Stores

We urge all colored people and fair minded white people to refuse to buy from any of the Peoples Drug Stores for the following reasons:

1. Peoples Drug Stores refuse to employ a single Negro clerk despite the fact that in several of these stores, according to our check, as high as 75 percent of the patronage is colored.

2. Colored people's money supports to a large degree these stores, but, despite this, colored people cannot even be served at the fountains as are other people.

3. The management of the Peoples Drug Stores has clearly indicated the belief that colored people are so lacking in self respect and intelligence that they will continue to pour their money into the pockets of those who not only insult them but who would keep at the lowest point their earning power.

YOUR MONEY TALKS!   *STICK TOGETHER!*
STAY OUT OF "PEOPLES"!

THE NEW NEGRO ALLIANCE.
Eugene Davidson, Chairman,   George H. Rycraw, Administrator.
Peoples Drug Stores Committee. Miss Arnetta L. Randall, Secretary.

Buy Where You Clerk!!

Above: Eugene Davidson, branch president from 1952 to 1958, pickets a Peoples Drug Store with other New Negro Alliance activists. Davidson began his civil rights activism with the NNA. *Moorland-Spingarn Research Center, Howard University.*

Left: New Negro Alliance flyer urging "all colored people and fair minded white people" to boycott Peoples Drug Stores. *Moorland-Spingarn Research Center, Howard University.*

to advocate for civil rights through direct economic activism. The NNA's birth was rooted in an August 28, 1933 incident when John Aubrey Davis, a twenty-one-year-old graduate of Williams College, and a group of his peers picketed the Hamburger Grill, a white-owned (but Black-supported) eatery on Twelfth and U Street NW for firing three African American employees and replacing them with white men. The group secured an effective and surprisingly easy victory. The Hamburger Grill closed the next day, quickly rehired the fired workers after the community boycotted the establishment at the urging of Davis's group and reopened four days later.[196]

The branch joined the NNA on some initiatives, including a 1934 meeting with the District commissioners that demanded an increase in people of color for the administration of New Deal government relief work and a fiery meeting in 1936 with Hecht's Department Store officials over its Jim Crow restroom policies that ended with shouted insults and threats of a boycott. By that time, fifty-two Black men and women had secured jobs due to the NNA's work at ten establishments in the city: American Stores, Atlantic and Pacific Tea Company, Brown's Corner, Capital Five and Ten Cents Store, Coney Island Barbecue, Epstein's Meat Market, High's Ice Cream, Hamburger Grill, Hollywood Shoe Store and Willis Cut-Rite Market. The branch, however, was not actively involved in these victories. Much to Davis's chagrin, Pinkett's conservatism characterized his description of the branch in the mid-1930s. It was "completely dominated by the respectable, well-off and stuffed-shirt residents of the city," he recalled in a 1982 interview. Deeming the NNA's strategies and picketing methods as too confrontational, the branch neither sanctioned them nor committed any direct cooperation. Leaders, supported by the membership, wanted no cooperation with what they characterized as "the rowdy element."[197]

A City with No Branch

By 1937, Bruce and Pinkett's "old guard" governance had created much tension with the more radical members who were also participating in the NNA's activities. The conflict reached its pinnacle at a three-hour meeting on January 15 at the Twelfth Street YMCA Building. A bitter election dispute resulted in a "left-wing group of about seventy" moving to another part of the hall and voting for officers of their own branch. Bruce and Pinkett were reelected president and secretary, garnering 240 and 231 votes respectively of the 250 who remained in the room. The factional members selected William H. Jernagin, pastor of Mount Carmel Baptist Church, to serve as their president, but there was one problem. He was not present and unaware of the vote until the *Afro* notified him. Acknowledging his awkward predicament, Jernagin was skeptical about the branch's future. "I am wondering though whether we are helping the cause of the NAACP by having two branches in Washington," he told the *Afro*.[198]

The controversy posed an obvious question. What would become of the NAACP in Washington? Burroughs expressed the fear that many had. "No branch—not even the National Association is strong enough to stand internal warfare," she wrote to NAACP executive secretary Walter White. For the second time in its history, a major conflict threatened to dismantle the organization. The Waldron era had returned. It was 1913 all over again.[199]

White called for a new election, but Bruce and Pinkett responded by filing an incorporation of the branch as its own entity in the Recorder of Deeds Office. The national office elevated the crisis by then revoking the branch's chapter through announcements in the *Washington Afro-American* and *Washington Tribune*. Additionally, it sought an injunction against the incorporated branch's name in the U.S. District Court for the District of Columbia, which Judge Thomas Jennings Bailey had approved, to prevent any solicitation or collection of funds. As a member of the branch and the national board, Charles Edward Russell attempted to mediate the controversy by urging a compromise but was unsuccessful. It was now official: the NAACP did not exist in Washington.[200]

The rift continued for two years. As a wave of police brutality incidents plagued the city, both sides finally met in the District Court to settle the conflict with Bailey serving as an arbitrator. Representing the national body, Charles Hamilton Houston and Thurgood Marshall huddled with Hayes and James Cobb, representatives of the branch, and established an agreement to ensure "that the work of the National Association for the Advancement of Colored People may go forward in the District of Columbia with unified effort and utmost vigor." The incorporated branch would be dissolved, the revocation of the charter would be rescinded, both parties would be responsible for their own legal fees and those elected in January 1937 would retain their offices until the next election. On January 17, 1939, U.S. District Court associate judge Daniel O'Donoghue ruled, "I find for the plaintiff, the facts in their bill have been substantially proven. I also find that the three defendants perpetrated a fraud on the national body." It was finally over.[201]

The branch's reemergence was gradual. In March, a special reorganization campaign was launched at First Christian Church at

Dear Former N.A.A.C.P. Member:

Reestablishment of the District of Columbia Branch will be started in a membership campaign under the direction of our Field Secretary, Mrs. Daisy E. Lampkin, on March 13. Headquarters of the campaign will be at the Y.M.C.A., 1816-12th Street Northwest.

The number and nature of the problems facing the citizens of Washington make it imperative that a large and effectively functioning branch be created immediately. May we count on your help not only by renewing your membership but by active participation in the drive. Will you get in touch with Mrs. Lampkin at drive headquarters?

Secretary

March 9, 1939.

Walter White was eager for the branch to reorganize after the 1937–39 dispute with the national office and sent these notices to former members. *DC History Center.*

Twelfth and S Streets NW. A committee selected C. Herbert Marshall, a prominent physician, to serve as temporary chairman. Daisy Lampkin returned to Washington to help lead a drive that targeted five thousand new members. By May, Marshall was elected president along with a new slate of officers and an executive committee, ushering out the conservative Bruce and Pinkett wing. The choice of Metropolitan AME Church for this rebirth was not lost on the membership as it was the same place where the branch organized in 1912. The revamped unit was praised by Russell, who attended as a guest speaker. It was "a new spirit of [the Black] race," he said. "Your group must fight for a principle which is essential to the continuation of civilization. There should be no changes, no differences because of race, but rather equality for all."[202]

The branch's transformation in the 1930s from the leading civil rights organization in the District to a conservative group whose implosion almost rendered it nonexistent came with a heavy price. It left a wide vacuum as the New Negro Alliance, National Negro Congress, Communist Party and other radical groups connected with Black Washingtonians of all classes, took up many of the battles the branch originally initiated and won impressive victories against them. In 1938, the Supreme Court ruled in *New Negro Alliance v. Sanitary Grocery Company* that the right to picket was constitutional. In response to several shootings of Black men that same year, the NNA and

Returning the branch to its glory as the leading civil rights organization in the District was Dr. C. Herbert Marshall's (*right*) main priority when he was elected its president in May 1939. *DC Public Library, Star Collection © Washington Post.*

the local Communist Party led a two-thousand-person march from Tenth and U Streets NW to Rhode Island Avenue and Ninth Street NW. The crowds, estimated between ten and fifteen thousand, witnessed marchers carrying signs that read "Washington Is Not Scottsboro" and "You May Be Next" and heard chants of "Stop Legal Lynching!" and "Police Brutality Must Go!" For all the branch's work against lynching and police violence, its presence at the march was minimal.[203]

In February 1939, when famed contralto singer Marian Anderson was denied permission by the Daughters of the American Revolution (DAR) to perform at Constitution Hall, the branch could do little more than pass a resolution of condemnation and encourage members to join the multiorganizational Marian Anderson Citizens Committee. That April, White wanted the branch to initiate a lawsuit against the DAR that would take away its tax-exempt status, but Marshall refused, citing the effort to rebuild and the desire to avoid any action that could jeopardize success. "We are only in temporary condition," he replied to White. "You realize the care

After being denied permission to perform at Constitution Hall by the Daughters of the American Revolution, famed contralto singer Marian Anderson performed at the Lincoln Memorial on Easter Sunday in 1939 before an integrated crowd of more than seventy-five thousand. *Library of Congress (LC-DIG-ppmsca-23838).*

that I must exercise at this time to prevent unnecessary, as well as unfair, criticism of the NAACP by those who are straining to find fault."[204]

The NNA claimed victory in December 1939 in opening the new Crosstown Drug Store at Fourteenth and U Streets NW directly opposite the Peoples Drug Store, which the Alliance boycotted for more than a year over its firm stance against the employment of Black clerks and pharmacists. A *Washington Tribune* editorial titled "Co-operation That Counts" lavished praise on the NNA and other groups in the city that were instrumental in securing "300 job opportunities" for African Americans. The branch was not included. It had attempted to achieve autonomy and hegemony over the national office but resulted only in an abdication of leadership to other organizations instead.[205]

Generational, gender and ideological changes affected the branch leadership and drastically shaped the organization for years. Five former, acting and current presidents died in the first four years of the decade (including John Milton Waldron in 1931 "after a long illness" and Carrie Clifford at her home in 1934 after a card game and dinner with friends). With the exception of Merritt, all were affiliated with the branch's founding. Virginia McGuire's presidency was the last by a woman; it would not be until the mid-1970s that another, Betty Holton, would be elected to the office. Some on the new executive committee, like future branch president Eugene Davidson, were former NNA officers and members determined to engage with all Black Washingtonians to conquer the city's racial woes, regardless of class. Returning the branch to its glory as the leading civil rights organization in Washington was now the top priority. Against the backdrop of a second world war in the 1940s, the forthcoming battles against school segregation in the 1950s provided ample opportunity.[206]

6

ON THE NATIONAL STAGE

*I*n 1951, Gardner Bishop's membership in the branch was unimaginable. A native of Rocky Mount, North Carolina, he was a champion high school debater and worked in his father's barbershop, shining shoes for white patrons. Some he liked, but most of them he despised. It was the small slights that angered him. When an influenza epidemic struck the city, Bishop's father closed his shop and barbered his customers in his home. These white men did not even have the courtesy to remove their hats until they climbed into the chair. What was worse was that young Gardner had a mouth on him, but he had to bite his tongue if he was going to remain in his father's good graces—and his house.[207]

Bishop had no love for the Black men in town either, especially the ministers who were considered the respected community leaders folks wanted to emulate. They cared little about demanding justice from the white man or spreading the faith and more about the success of their churches. Bishop attended Shaw University in Raleigh for one year, came to Washington in 1930 and got a job in a white barbershop. He did not last long. A racist joke from one of his patrons was countered by Bishop with a tale in which the white man was the fool. That was the end of him working in that world. In 1940, he opened the B&D Shop in the 1500 block of the District's famed African American corridor and became "the U Street barber." Bishop felt at home. He proudly served a clientele he could identify with: The guys who shot craps to make money. The fatherless children who became vandals instead of students. The drunks and the addicts. The street people who "Bish," as his friends called him, believed the Black NAACP establishment wanted to disown and the white establishment wanted gone from the city. "It was double Jim Crow," Bishop described the perpetrators in both races.[208]

Recreational segregation was an important fight for the branch in the 1940s, but the legal victories over school segregation in the 1950s included District cases to which the branch was connected. The long path to *Brown v. Board of Education of Topeka* began in the spring of 1947 in Washington, and Bishop was a part of it all. His daughter, Judine, was a student at Hugh M. Browne Junior High School. Named after Hugh M. Browne (1851–1923), a native Washingtonian and

Gardner Bishop outside his B&D barbershop at Fifteenth and U Streets NW. *DC Public Library, Star Collection © Washington Post.*

educator, it opened in 1932 as the first junior high school in the "colored division" in Northeast Washington. Its original construction was for 888 students, but by the time America entered World War II, Browne was significantly overcrowded with 1,462 students. In the postwar era, it was the most overcrowded school in the entire city and served as the starkest example of inequality in Washington's public education system.[209]

CORNING V. CARR

By February 1947, Browne's student body was 1,707, more than double the building's capacity. Charles W. Eliot Junior High School, a new school for white students, was constructed near Browne in 1931. By the 1940s, it had plenty of unused space, as many white parents placed their children in private schools or moved to the Maryland and Virginia suburbs. The parents in the Browne Parent-Teacher Association believed that petitioning the Board of Education to transfer the students to Eliot in order to alleviate the overcrowding was an easy solution. The petition was filed against

Hobart Corning served as superintendent of DC Public Schools from 1946 to 1958. *DC Public Library, Star Collection © Washington Post.*

Superintendent Hobart Corning on behalf of Marguerite Daisy Carr, the daughter of PTA president James C. Carr Sr.[210]

It yielded no success. Corning acknowledged the school's deficiencies in an official report but opposed the transfer of students. Representing the branch as the chair of its legal committee, Leon Ransom reported back to the Board of Education that Corning's "so-called 'report'…admits all the major promises of the complaint, but fails to make any specific recommendations from the relief desired." The branch supported a lawsuit against Corning, and the Browne PTA held a mass meeting to garner support and financial contributions. Bishop reluctantly attended. He was not a PTA member. He had never even attended a meeting. The members were not his people. They were the same who ran the NAACP, the educated professionals with the high-salaried government jobs who lived in the fancy neighborhoods. Even the grandiose manner in which they spoke turned Bishop off, like how Belford Lawson, an attorney who worked with the New Negro Alliance in the 1930s, explained the case and legal strategy at the meeting. Neither he nor the parents were impressed. The case was going to be unsuccessful,

Bishop predicted, "but nobody asked us what we thought because we were nothin'! Nobody gave us a chance to speak. What we wanted was relief, not lawsuits with $500 fees."[211]

Ransom and his law partner, Austin L. Fickling, filed the suit *Corning v. Carr* in the U.S. District Court of the District of Columbia on October 7, 1947. The case moved slowly through the courts, and parents lost patience as they realized the litigation could take years. School officials proposed a solution to the overcrowding that pushed the parents to agitation through civil disobedience: the transfer of the dilapidated Henry T. Blow and William B. Webb Elementary Schools to the "colored division" to serve as annexes to Browne. The conditions were deplorable. Neither school had an auditorium, library, gymnasium or cafeteria. The male teachers at Webb

Leon Ransom, Howard Law School professor and head of the branch's Legal Committee, filed *Carr v. Corning* in 1947 against Superintendent Corning for opposing the transfer of Black students at Hugh Browne Junior High School to the all-white Charles W. Eliot Junior High School to alleviate overcrowding. *DC Public Library, Star Collection © Washington Post.*

had no bathroom facilities, and there were no lounges for the Blow teachers. Three Blow classrooms had damaged blackboards, and both schools had broken windowpanes. Distance was also problematic: Blow was seven blocks from Browne, and Webb was located fifteen blocks away. Parents were appalled. "The average parent does not give a hoot about his child going to a white school, but he does not want the fact that his child must be segregated used as an excuse for his being given sub-standard…school facilities abandoned by whites," argued parent and activist Nellie V. Greene.[212]

Bolling v. Sharpe and Brown v. Board

It was time to take a bold stand. At the first meeting of what became the Browne Parent Group for Equality of Educational Opportunities, more than 160 parents, led by Greene and Capitol View Civic Association leader Joy Davis, signed a petition at Jones Memorial Methodist Church to keep their children out of school until there was "adequate relief from part-time schooling." Bishop served as spokesperson, but the makeup of the group with regard to class and gender contradicted his characterization of the strike as the "little people" against the "big people." The majority of the parents were homeowners, and the largest group of workers were in the federal government or private industries. Several were also self-employed like Bishop, including two pharmacists and one spiritualist.[213]

The strike began on December 3, 1947. Parents picketed both the board's offices at the Franklin School and Browne, but criticism from school officials demoralized the parents. The branch was placed in an awkward position. Some parents were skeptical of its support. George E.C. Hayes was appointed to the board in February 1945 while also serving as branch president. As a member, he now opposed the strike. "We should inveigh against segregation whenever possible but I do not think that as a minority group we have a right to ask that law be enforced by violating it," he argued.[214]

The branch sought to turn the parents' waning interest in the strike into an opportunity to present a united legal front. A "suit to be brought through the sponsorship of NAACP with the financial and moral support of the PTA, all parent groups and the community" was the goal, according to several meeting notes. Bishop ventured into enemy territory by going to a meeting. These "high falutin" Black folk were the last people he wanted to be around, but he needed their help. Fortunately, he met Charles Hamilton Houston, and they hit it off immediately. Houston filed a suit on his behalf that focused on equalizing resources in schools for Black and white students. In *Bishop et. al. v. Doyle*, Houston did not challenge desegregation directly since the Fourteenth Amendment's promise of equal treatment pertained to violations of citizens' rights by state governments.[215]

Houston's approach resulted only in a partial victory. The board annexed four other buildings (Webb, Blow, Turner Elementary and Merritt Elementary) to Browne to allow students to attend classes, but in February 1950, the *Carr* case was unsuccessful. Just as Bishop had predicted, the U.S. District Court of Appeals ruled in a 2–1 decision that the "separate but equal" theory for education was valid. Judges Bernett Champ Clark and E. Barrett Prettyman wrote in their majority opinion: "Constitutional invalidity does not arise from the mere fact of separation, but may arise from an inequality of treatment." Judge Henry W. Edgerton's lone dissent mirrored Supreme Court justice John Harlan's 1896 minority *Plessy* opinion that the Constitution was intended to be colorblind. "Equal protection of the laws is not achieved through indiscriminate imposition of inequalities," he wrote. "It is plain that pupils represented in these appeals are denied better schooling and given worse because of their color." Ransom and his team presented arguments for an appeal to the court, but the justices declined to hear the case.[216]

Houston died two months later of a heart attack, but not before suggesting to Bishop and his group (now the Consolidated Parent Group, or CPG) to reach out to his Howard Law School colleague and friend James Nabrit Jr. to carry on the work of multiple equalization cases. Nabrit agreed to represent them, but only if they agreed to confront desegregation directly. The equalization approach, he advised, was futile and had run its course. They complied. Now all that was needed was a test case.[217]

They found one in Spottswood Thomas Bolling Jr., an eleven-year-old student at Shaw Junior High School. In September 1950, Bishop took a group of eleven Black schoolchildren, including Spottswood, to enroll in the new, all-white John Philip Sousa Junior High School in Southeast Washington. There was plenty of space for the Black students, as many of the forty-two classrooms were empty. Sousa also had a six-hundred-seat auditorium, a double gymnasium, a softball field and a playground with seven basketball courts. Its location across the street from a plush golf course made it even more pristine. Spottswood's widowed mother, Sarah, a bookbinder at the federal General Services Administration, wanted the best for her son, as did the other parents. Their school was forty-eight years old, dingy, ill-equipped, located near a pawnbroker's shop and had a science laboratory that comprised one Bunsen burner and a bowl of goldfish. How could anyone get an education at a place like that? Who would want to?[218]

School officials, led by Board of Education president C. Melvin Sharpe and Black assistant superintendent Garnet Wilkinson (who also served as the branch's treasurer in the 1930s), proposed the use of the crumbling Birney School instead of integrating Sousa. It triggered an angry response from parents. "Dual systems have never produced equality and the general rule is the colored child always bears the brunt of inequalities," Bishop told the board, on behalf of the CPG. In early 1951, Nabrit and Hayes filed *Bolling v. Sharpe* in U.S. District Court.[219]

Hayes's branch presidency and Nabrit's chairmanship of its legislation and legal address committee connected the organization to *Bolling*, but it ended there. Bishop was a member by this time, but he believed the NAACP was still too much of a "social group" and feared its presence would only jeopardize a successful outcome. Heeding Bishop's request, Nabrit and Hayes worked on the case independently. However, the branch took the

Above: An ardent foe of the branch, South Carolina congressman John McMillan served for decades on the House District Committee, where he slashed budgets for Black schools and strongly opposed home rule. *DC Public Library, Star Collection © Washington Post.*

Opposite: City affairs were governed by the congressional House District of Columbia Committee from 1808 to 1995. White southerners dominated the committee for many years, treating the District like a plantation. *DC Public Library, Star Collection © Washington Post.*

school desegregation fight to Congress. In June 1952, Representative John "Johnny Mac" McMillan, a South Carolina Democrat and ardent segregationist, introduced a bill authorizing $5 million to improve conditions at existing Black schools and also construct new ones. It was condemned by the branch. In a letter to the House District Committee, officials described the bill as "an expenditure of funds designed to duplicate space already existing in the schools which should be made available to all the children in the District of Columbia without credence to race, creed, or color." The branch made national news. Mary McLeod Bethune, founder of the National Council of Negro Women, chastised McMillan's legislation as "blood money" and "another Klan march to the pulpits!" District commissioner F. Joseph Donahue charged that Sharpe's audacity to even request an appropriation from a member of Congress was "illegal." Pressure from the branch ultimately prevented its passage, but Sharpe and McMillan's efforts illustrated just how far officials were willing to go to preserve segregated education in the capital.[220]

The U.S. District Court dismissed *Bolling*, prompting Nabrit and Hayes to appeal to the Supreme Court on December 10, 1952. The case was combined with four others in Delaware, Kansas, South Carolina and Virginia that comprised *Brown v. Board*. The NAACP attorneys, led by future Supreme Court justice Thurgood Marshall, argued the Fourteenth Amendment guaranteed equal protection under the law and segregation violated the United Nations' charter on human rights. By comparison, Nabrit and Hayes's argument was less complex: school officials simply had no authority to reject students' entry into Sousa on the basis of race.[221]

Sarah Bolling embraces her son Spottswood T. Bolling in their home after the U.S. Supreme Court's 1954 *Brown vs. Board* ruling invalidated segregated schools. *DC Public Library, Star Collection © Washington Post.*

It was impossible to predict how the court would rule, but on June 8, 1953, it signaled hope. In a unanimous decision in *District of Columbia v. John R. Thompson Co. Inc.*, the court ended segregation in all businesses, including restaurants. Mary Church Terrell had led a sit-in demonstration at Thompson's Restaurant, a public cafeteria at 725 Fourteenth Street NW, several blocks from the Eisenhower White House, on January 27, 1950. As members of the Coordinating Committee for the Enforcement of the D.C. Antidiscrimination Laws, the group needed a discrimination case to test the validity of the 1872 "Lost Laws." They found one at Thompson's.[222]

Activists endured pickets, bouts with the pro-segregationist Washington Restaurant Association and appeals in the lower courts before the justices ruled that the Reconstruction-era laws "remain today…a part of the governing body of laws applicable to the District." Terrell and some friends returned to Thompson's to celebrate. The manager served them. "I will die happy to know that the children of my group will not grow up thinking they are inferior because they are deprived of rights which children of other racial groups enjoy," she triumphantly declared. Would the Court reach the same conclusion with *Bolling*?[223]

On May 17, 1954, it did. In a 550-word opinion in *Brown v. Board*, Chief Justice Earl Warren wrote, "We hold that racial segregation in the

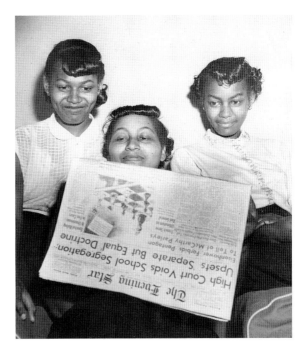

Barbara Jennings (*left*) and her sister Adrienne read the news about the *Brown* decision in the *Washington Evening Star* with their mother. *DC Public Library, Star Collection © Washington Post.*

public schools of the District of Columbia is a denial of the due process of law guaranteed by the Fifth Amendment to the Constitution." Sarah Bolling was elated, announcing triumphantly, "Now we can hold up our heads before the world." The historic moment was "a wonderful thing for this country."[224]

There were some positive results from *Brown* in the capital. Several schools integrated immediately, especially those that had been all-white. Out of its 163 schools, 122 were biracial after the decision. Overcrowding also lessened, albeit slightly. In 1952, the majority of Division Two school classrooms contained 40 to 44 students; by 1955, the range was 35 to 39. Nevertheless, the changes were piecemeal. Corning's desegregation plan presented a challenge. The superintendent submitted a proposal for "gradual" integration eight days after the ruling. Integration would be complete by September 1955. Until then, Black and white students would remain in their present schools from the elementary level to high school. Children entering school for the first time would be admitted to the one nearest to their home until zoning plans could be finalized to accommodate full integration. Corning also allowed for "hardship transfers" that were not to be based on race, but on the difficulty of students getting to school.[225]

Eugene Davidson Becomes Branch President

By this time, the branch was under the leadership of another Davidson. Eugene Davidson, the son of Executive Secretary Shelby Davidson, was elected in December 1952. Leading NNA pickets against People's Drug Store chains in the 1930s, forming the Washington Civil Rights Committee in 1940 and directing robust branch membership drives to end recreational segregation reflected his grassroots activism and dedication to civil rights. The surname certainly was an asset, too; the Davidsons were prominent in Black Washington, and other famed leaders held them in high regard. W.E.B. Du Bois was a close friend and often stayed at their home during visits to the city. In November 1951, Du Bois went on trial in the District on charges that he failed to register his defunct, New York–based Peace Information Center as a foreign agent. *Afro-American* columnist Louis Latimer sniped that despite Du Bois's support of the branch since the 1920s, Davidson and former executive secretary Archibald Pinkett were the only members to show up to the courtroom in solidarity.[226]

Davidson dismissed Corning's plan as a "mere token response" to *Brown* and vowed to muster the resources of the branch (and the national office if necessary) to fight the superintendent's "so-called orderly integration." In a letter to the Board of Education, Davidson and Ellis O. Knox, chair of the branch's education committee, attacked Corning's plan as what President Eisenhower did not envision when he "expressed hope that our school system would be a model for the country." It was imperative, they urged, "that desegregation here proceed without the obstacles of imaginary and unrealistic administrative difficulties." Testimony was more moving than words on paper, so Davidson invited frustrated parents who complained to the branch to berate board members at public hearings. Most protested the transfers. "I had to go all the way to the superintendent's office to get my boy transferred from Douglass Junior High School to a school two blocks from me," growled an angry mother. In a December 1955 branch report, Davidson signaled his intent to combat this new type of resistance that embodied Corning's philosophy and proposals. The old gradualism, which Davidson likened to "the train traveling to the promised land of democracy, but traveling very slowly even though steadily," had been replaced with something more intolerable. The new approach "permits the train to travel fast, but at every…station it stops and waits while the travelers forget the goal."[227]

Martin Luther King Jr. and the 1957 Prayer Pilgrimage for Freedom

Much had not changed by the ruling's third anniversary in May 1957. Integration was still moving "with all deliberate speed," as mandated by the court due to a wave of "massive resistance" efforts by segregationist politicians in the South. This issue, along with the gruesome lynching of Emmett Till in Mississippi, the Montgomery, Alabama bus boycott and a civil rights bill languishing in Congress, shaped the struggles that would become the civil rights movement of the 1960s. The commemoration of *Brown*, coupled with the failure of the Eisenhower administration to move against anti-Black violence in the South and make a bold commitment to desegregation, led civil rights leaders to organize a "Prayer Pilgrimage for Freedom" at the Lincoln Memorial. On April 5, 1957, A. Philip Randolph, Ella Baker, Bayard Rustin, NAACP executive secretary Roy Wilkins and Martin Luther King Jr. met at Metropolitan Baptist Church at 1225 R Street NW to finalize plans. Nannie Helen Burroughs, a close friend of King's parents and mentor to young Martin, who also loved him like a son, was invited. Their religious work and Baptist organizational memberships connected them, and Burroughs was putting him in front of her audiences as early as August 1954, when he was just twenty-five.[228]

It is difficult to document the first time King came to the capital. However, he placed the branch on the national stage of the emerging civil rights movement with one of his earliest visits, which preceded the pilgrimage. The aspiring pastor of Dexter Avenue Baptist Church touted the importance of the Montgomery Improvement Association's bus boycott at Howard University's Andrew Rankin Memorial Chapel on December 7, 1956. The yearlong campaign was the result of a new generation's resistance. "The new Negro lacks the fear he once had and he has a new sense of dignity," King preached to his audience in a sermon titled "Remember Who You Are!" Black southerners were justifiably fed up, he said. "There comes a time when people get tired of being trampled by the iron foot of oppression." King left the campus and took his message all over the city, wrapping up at the branch's meeting at Vermont Avenue Baptist Church that night with an address on "Facing the Challenge of a New Age." He was exhausted, but he had reached about four thousand Washingtonians. Not bad for a single day.[229]

On the morning of the pilgrimage, King, Wilkins and Randolph, accompanied by Davidson, met with District commissioner Robert

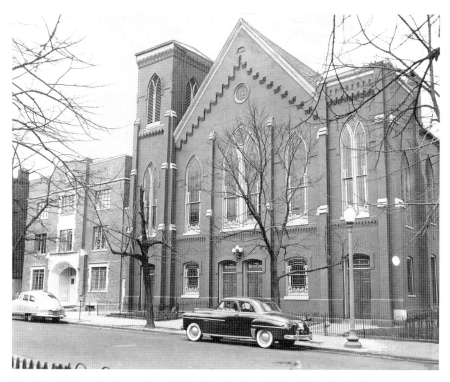

Branch officials and other national civil rights leaders finalized plans for the Prayer Pilgrimage for Freedom at Metropolitan Baptist Church in the Logan Circle–Shaw neighborhood. *DC Public Library, Star Collection © Washington Post.*

McLaughlin, who presented the trio with a key to the city. The three-hour event, marked by prayers, songs and speeches, began at noon with a magnificent wreath laid at Lincoln's feet by seven-year-old Theresa Gordon and her ten-year-old brother, James, of Clay, Kentucky, to honor children who had integrated schools nationally. The siblings had attempted to enroll in an all-white school but were met with threats of violence. The family was forced to flee Kentucky. Then came the speeches. Congressman Adam Clayton Powell, a fiery Democrat from New York, attacked the "basic dishonesty and increasing hypocrisy of our two political parties" and claimed they were at the Lincoln Memorial "because we are getting more from a dead Republican than we are from getting from live Democrats and live Republicans."[230]

King, whose newly formed Southern Christian Leadership Conference enabled him to serve as the Prayer Pilgrimage's co-chair, concluded the program with a rousing address equal to Powell's in its passion but devoid

A. Philip Randolph, Roy Wilkins and Martin Luther King Jr. receive the key to the city from Commissioner Robert McLaughlin on the morning of the Prayer Pilgrimage. Branch president Eugene Davidson (*not pictured*) accompanied the group. *DC Public Library, Star Collection © Washington Post.*

of its abrasiveness. In a call-and-response fashion, King demanded, "Give us the ballot!" with the crowd chanting the phrase in return. His presence in front of the "Great Emancipator" was the first time many in the crowd had seen him. Observers hailed the moment as a significant turning point for King. The youthful minister, wrote *New York Amsterdam News* editor James Hicks, had emerged as "the number one leader of sixteen million Negroes in the United States. At this point, the people will follow him everywhere."[231]

As the "coordinator of efforts by the national committee" and a member of the local arrangements committee, Davidson had no choice but to put a positive spin on the event. "I think the Pilgrimage was a wonderful success. I never saw anything so inspiring," he told the *Afro-American*. It was certainly a success in that there were no protests by Communists, as organizers had feared. Nor was there any unruly behavior, which some officials thought would be sensationalized by the white press. Edward P. Morgan of the

Martin Luther King Jr. at the Prayer Pilgrimage with A. Philip Randolph and Roy Wilkins. *DC Public Library, Star Collection © Washington Post.*

American Broadcasting Company said, "No [segregationist Mississippi] Senator Eastland was hanged in effigy." Organizers were relieved.[232]

Many outsiders thought it was a success too. Grady Cummings, a twenty-three-year-old messenger from Harlem, was surprised when he first arrived in Washington a week before the Pilgrimage. "Man this town is dead," he thought, as he saw no "sound trucks in the streets" blasting out details about the march. "We have been talking up this meeting in Harlem for weeks." With less than two weeks to prepare, Davidson had to speed up efforts to put out the welcome mat. Washington finally came alive with sound trucks, homes offered to strangers who could not find hotel rooms and similar accommodations coordinated by twenty-five churches and other organizations.[233]

At the same time, the rosy prediction that more than fifty thousand would attend did not materialize. Only twenty-five to thirty thousand came and "just about ten thousand from Washington," according to Davidson. Although upbeat, he did not hold back his frustration in his reasoning for the low turnout. Having the event at noon was a mistake, he said. "If I had made the decision, I would have set the time…around 5:30 p.m. It's hard in many cases for government workers to take off from their jobs." Davidson also thought a Saturday or Sunday would have been more prudent instead of a weekday. An extensive sample of government workers, grocery clerks, filling station attendants, bank cashiers, hairdressers, housewives, students, shoeshine boys and insurance supervisors interviewed by the *Afro* confirmed Davidson's conclusions. An anonymous U Street pharmacist was blunt: "Making a living was more important." Others feared they would violate

Howard University president Mordecai Johnson was the only person from Washington to address the Prayer Pilgrimage. Branch leaders were excluded from the official list of speakers. *Library of Congress (LC-DIG-hec-24272).*

the Hatch Act if they attended, and some of the no-shows were simply attributed to childish behavior. Ethel Payne, a *Chicago Defender* journalist, reported in her regular "So…This Is Washington" column that "one prominent cleric who could have [brought] at least 5,000 of the faithful got piqued because he wasn't asked to be on the program and left the morning of the pilgrimage."[234]

Privately, Davidson fumed about something that probably was not lost on the attendees: the branch's lack of representation among the speakers. Davidson handled local arrangements, but Wilkins muzzled him and other branch officials on the stage. The only speaker from the District was Howard University president Mordecai Johnson. He made regular guest speaker appearances at branch meetings but on this day spoke eloquently—and extensively—about the necessity of both political parties "to stop doing the things that are unholy."[235]

Just two women spoke at the Pilgrimage, and neither was from Washington. Vivian Carter Mason of Norfolk, Virginia, and Irene McCoy Gaines of Chicago, presidents of the National Council of Negro Women and National Association of Colored Women's Clubs, respectively, addressed the crowd, but Burroughs should have been up there too. It is unknown if she was invited to speak or, at the age of seventy-eight, was physically unable to participate. Burroughs had held anti-lynching prayer meetings at various Washington churches as early as 1917, and she had supported King and the Alabama NAACP long before the Pilgrimage. In February 1956, she donated twenty-five dollars to support the Montgomery Bus Boycott. That September, aware that Black teachers in Alabama risked being fired in retaliation for their involvement with the NAACP, Burroughs offered to hire them to work at her National Training School for Girls and Women.[236]

King did not know how much his presence and words had emboldened the branch. His "Give us the ballot!" calls as a means to securing anti-lynching legislation and confronting "the salient misdeeds of blood-thirsty mobs" were interpreted by members as references to police brutality. The rising leader also helped engage more Washingtonians with the branch's work. "I'm in favor of the NAACP 100 percent. It's doing a good job," said Alexander Williams, a self-employed resident of Northwest Washington. "We need more men like Rev. Martin Luther King."[237]

1957 Metropolitan Police Department Complaint

Instances of brutality in the Metropolitan Police Department had declined in the 1940s but escalated in the next decade. "One of the most heinous and reprehensible" cases occurred in July 1953 when two police officers were tipped off to investigate a false 3:00 a.m. disorderly conduct call at the home of thirty-eight-year-old Mildred Green and her seven-year-old son. They accused her of being drunk and broke her arm when they dragged her down

Eugene Davidson, branch president from 1952 to 1958. *DC Public Library, Star Collection © Washington Post.*

a flight of stairs while her little boy slept. "I was hysterical," she told the *Afro*, upon arriving at Precinct 14 on drunk and disorderly conduct charges. The officers faced no disciplinary action.[238]

By 1956, Davidson was constantly getting "unsatisfactory" correspondence from MPD chief Robert Murray regarding inquiries of police shootings of unarmed Black men arrested for misdemeanors. Very few officers were indicted by District Court grand juries, and those who were never saw a trial or conviction. Murray's Police Board also never took disciplinary action. Davidson often turned to McLaughlin, who supervised the police, but rarely was he even granted a meeting. Employment and hiring were also troubling. Julius Hobson, a Birmingham, Alabama native and former vice president of the Federation of Civic Associations, joined the branch in 1957 as a member of the executive committee and chair of its employment committee. In a report by the National Association of Intergroup Relations Officials' Commission on Civil Rights, Hobson utilized his skills as a Library of Congress researcher and Social Security Administration statistician to cite disturbing figures about the department. Just 11 percent of its 2,100 members was Black. All 199 deputy chiefs, inspectors, captains, lieutenants and sergeants were white.[239]

On June 6, 1957, Davidson called for Murray's ouster before an audience at the Capitol Press Club. The chief's dismissal of the branch's complaints over brutality was indicative that he was "more interested in protecting his men than protecting citizens' rights," Davidson said. That, coupled with the lack of promotion of Black officers, made for a "dangerous policy." Davidson took his proposal to Hobson and the rest of the executive committee. Upon approval, he formally presented the branch's resolution to the District commissioners, seeking a hearing. Murray disputed the charges, telling the *Star* that his unblemished record of "five and one-half years" spoke for itself and that he would "use the personnel in a way in which I feel I can render the best police service to the citizens of the District and visitors to the Capitol."[240]

The branch filed a formal complaint alleging discrimination and police brutality against Metropolitan Police Department chief Robert Murray in June 1957. The commissioners exonerated Murray in November 1957. *DC Public Library, Star Collection © Washington Post.*

Murray wanted the matter to be dropped quickly. It was fruitless for the commissioners to consider the branch's "very serious…in my opinion, libelous" accusations, he stated. If he was going to appear at any hearing though, he wanted "a bill of particulars with names, dates, times, and places, so that I will not have to deal with generalities." McLaughlin, who would have the final decision on a hearing, wanted specifics as well, but not before he prematurely voiced support for the chief who has been "made the subject of…general and unsubstantial charges." He also rejected Davidson's request for the charges to be heard by a panel of distinguished and impartial Washingtonians selected by the branch. Davidson agreed that "Mr. Murray is entitled to a bill of particulars and one will be forthcoming."[241]

The branch issued a thorough "Information in the Nature of Partial Documentation Particulars and Evidence in the Matter of Metropolitan Police Department and Chief Robert V. Murray" in July. The twenty-four-page document was anything but partial. Packed with quantitative data

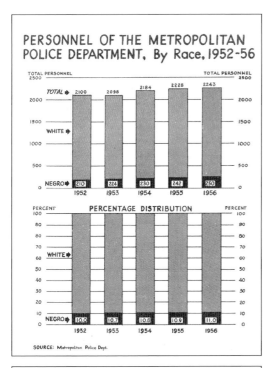

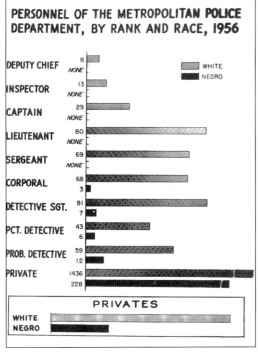

The branch used these 1956 MPD statistics to support its discrimination complaint. *DC Public Library.*

supplied by Hobson on the bleak percentage of African American personnel, the complaint was also strongly balanced with affidavits and testimony from Black Washingtonians who had been brutalized by white officers. Some accounts included graphic photographs illustrating the aftermath of near-fatal encounters. One vivid example was Isaac Williams Jr., who had been arrested on a disorderly conduct charge. The file included a photograph of Williams's head that showed marks from adhesive bandages and stitches. The department claimed he had injured himself when he fell down the Fifth Precinct stairs while handcuffed to another escorting officer. The photograph told a different story, and so did Williams. Yes, he had fallen, but "I was propped up against the wall…and Officer L.A. Hines struck me in the head first." Ada Mae Brown, a Southeast resident, was waiting for a bus when two officers shouted at her to get in a scout car, "cursed her, and hit her with a blackjack." The officers were not done with her at the police station. By the time it was over, Brown had a broken shoulder and jawbone and thirteen stitches in her mouth.[242]

The branch's complaint galvanized much of Black Washington. Letters of support from many business, political and religious organizations that comprised the Federation of Civic Associations poured into the commissioners' offices in late July. With so much opposition against Murray, Davidson was compelled to urge the Federal Bureau of Investigation to probe the department. It was no longer an issue of individual complaints. "The whole police department needs to be changed," Davidson said. "There are so many things Chief Murray could have done to eliminate police brutality." Warren Olney III, assistant attorney general in charge of the criminal division, declined the request, stating it was in the interests of his office to investigate civil rights violations and not individual cases of brutality. What Davidson wanted was something Olney would not pursue. "The FBI is not in the business of making surveys of police departments."[243]

By October, the hearings were scheduled to begin. McLaughlin had a public relations crisis on his hands. He still regarded the complaint as nothing more than a personal attack on Murray, and he did not want the branch's pressure on his office to "further fan the flames." McLaughlin tried a final, desperate attempt to seek an amicable solution on the hearings' first day. Thirty minutes before the first witness was called in the District Building, branch counsel Thurman L. Dodson and Roger Robb, Murray's attorney, huddled behind closed doors for a meeting arranged by McLaughlin and Corporation Counsel Chester E. Gray. A proposal was presented. If the charges were dropped, the commissioners would consult

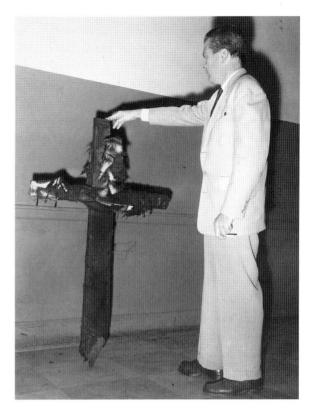

A *Washington Star* reporter "with Dixie leanings" inspects a wooden cross burned outside of Eugene Davidson's home in the early morning hours of October 2, 1957. Davidson laughed off the incident, adding, "I'm not afraid." *DC Public Library, Star Collection © Washington Post.*

with the branch on racial abuse allegations in the department and with the public. Dodson refused the compromise. The commissioners simply could not be trusted to deliver on that promise.[244]

The hearings lasted several days. Experts, officers, victims and community leaders testified on the condition of the police department and its practices. Murray defended himself and the department, especially on race and assignments. Men were selected on merit, he said, and neither the NAACP nor any other organization would dictate those assignments. Of the 280 black members of the department, 106 had been appointed by him. "I think I've promoted more colored men since I've been chief…than were promoted in the entire preceding 21 years." Some of the branch's last-minute "surprise" witnesses offered conflicting testimony. Henry R. Chase, a sanitary engineering employee, told NAACP counsel E. Lewis Ferrell how he was busted up by an officer. He bled from his mouth and head and, demonstrating how, told Ferrell, "Well his blackjack hit me up in here and my tooth came through my lip." Robb pounced, producing a statement Chase signed (most likely out of coercion) and read it into the record. It stated Ferrell had not wished to press any charges because "it was just a misunderstanding." Apparently, Ferrell "thought the motor-man was a Perfect Gentleman."[245]

Instances like Ferrell's were few, but the *Star* and *Post* used them to overshadow the testimonies of more credible witnesses and further discredit the branch's case. Both newspapers had published pro-Murray editorials as early as July, and the bombardment of criticism did not bode well for the branch in the court of public opinion. So it was no surprise that the commissioners found "no evidence whatever" in the validity of the charges and exonerated Murray on November 7. "On the other hand," they said, "the evidence submitted by Chief Murray completely answered the charges and specifications." Davidson responded that the decision "was expected" but also added that "it was further incredible and significant that the Commissioners concluded there are no weaknesses in the Police Department and ignored reasonable recommendations of the NAACP for improvement."[246]

Although Murray survived, the branch's case had shed light on the department's discriminatory practices and corruption. By 1959, there were some changes. A large percentage of Black plainclothes detectives were promoted. Six officers became sergeants and precinct and probationary detectives. The homicide squad gained two Black detectives, and several became health inspectors. At one point, a Black man served as acting head of the bureau, albeit "for a short period." Washingtonians also saw visible changes in police presence in their neighborhoods that were once unfathomable. Black officers now sat behind the steering wheels of police cruisers in predominately white Precincts 9, 14, and 19, and integrated squad cars were everywhere. And gone were the days in which officers collected funds to support and maintain segregated Police Boys Clubs.[247]

The Beginning of the Branch's Decline

Despite these improvements, many were dissatisfied, particularly Hobson. He dismissed the changes as tepid and unsatisfactory. In 1960, he noted that there were only 333 African American uniformed officers in the department out of 2,602, representing just 12.8 percent. In a city that became majority Black in 1957, those numbers should have been much higher. Hobson faulted the branch more than the commissioners for the outcome. So did the *Star*. Taking direct aim at its leaders, the newspaper editorialized:

"The Negro citizen in Washington needs forthright leadership by men and women willing to take the dangerous job of speaking up for [the] disadvantaged, while demanding justice and equal treatment." Hobson probably agreed with that conclusion, for it definitely was not living up to that role. It was too conservative. Too nonconfrontational. Missing was the radicalism that Carter G. Woodson desired in 1912, Thomas embodied in the 1920s and Burroughs advocated for in the 1930s. However, these individuals never abandoned the branch. Hobson was willing to consider that option. Perhaps this organization was not for him anymore.[248]

In the 1960s, King greatly influenced the civil rights struggles in Washington. However, in the 1950s, the branch's work shaped him as his goals and agenda for a national campaign emerged in the capital. Just nine days after the Pilgrimage, the Capital Press Club bestowed King with an award for his work with the MIA and his rousing address at the Lincoln Memorial. Unable to return to Washington to receive the honor, King could have designated anyone to accept it on his behalf. With Vice President Richard Nixon and the second lady looking on admiringly, *Washington Afro-American* managing editor Samuel Hoskins presented it to Davidson. On June

The description of the branch's service in this 1955 report as "militant" was oxymoronic, as it never adopted radical approaches to challenges facing Black Washingtonians. *DC Public Library.*

Above: Eugene Davidson accepts a plaque awarded to Martin Luther King Jr. from the Capital Press Club as *Washington Afro-American* editor Samuel Hoskins, Vice President Richard Nixon and Second Lady Pat Nixon look on. *DC Public Library, Star Collection © Washington Post.*

Left: E. Franklin Jackson, pastor of John Wesley AME Zion Church, served as branch president from 1959 to 1964. *DC Public Library, Star Collection © Washington Post.*

23, 1958, King and several leaders met with Eisenhower to present a nine-point plan for ending white supremacy and racism in the South and gaining full citizenship. The planning session with Randolph, Wilkins and National Urban League leader Lester B. Granger the day before could have been held anywhere in the city, but King chose the branch headquarters. He showed up with the others at 9:00 p.m., and the group burned the midnight oil, not departing until 4:00 a.m.[249]

On Sunday, December 15, 1957, members listened to Davidson's "State of the National Capital" report at Turner Memorial AME Church at Sixth and I Streets NW, timed to coincide with the 166th anniversary of the ratification of the Bill of Rights. Many applauded the branch's "great progress...made in the elimination of discrimination and segregation of public schools, public recreation, and places of amusement." On law enforcement specifically, the organization improved on the work from the 1930s and attributed this to Davidson's leadership. After nearly twenty years of making good trouble, he chose not to seek another presidential term in December 1958 and was succeeded by Edward Franklin Jackson, pastor of John Wesley Church, in January 1959. As national NAACP board member (and former branch official) W. Montague Cobb swore in the new president and Executive Committee, he urged members to "help Dr. Jackson raise your membership from 6,000 to 60,000." Davidson also made impassioned pleas of support for the branch and its new head. "I will be a worker, like you for the NAACP under its new president, the Rev. E. Franklin Jackson," he told the Athens Lodge's Amazon Club 8.[250]

From its birth in 1912, the branch was the leading organization in the apparatus of civil rights in the District of Columbia despite occasional battles within its ranks over demands to move in a more radical direction. However, the 1950s marked the end of that reign. As the SCLC, CORE and SNCC offered competing philosophies and strategies for the attainment of civil rights and the Black Power Movement elevated its voice, the branch's influence in the city waned significantly.

7

JOUSTING PHILOSOPHIES AND THE TRIUMPH OF BLACK POWER

*J*ulius Hobson exemplified the disillusionment that many Black Washingtonians would have with the branch in the 1960s. When he received a telephone call from Paul Bennett, a Black physicist and chairman of the District chapter of the Congress of Racial Equality (CORE), he knew he had made the right decision. Bennett needed someone to take control of the chapter. Was Hobson interested? It would not be an easy task. Founded in 1942 by James Farmer in Chicago, CORE was an interracial organization whose Washington chapter had few members and little influence in the city. Its principles arose from Mohandas K. Gandhi's philosophy of nonviolence, but Hobson agreed to lead the chapter on the condition that nonviolence would be a strategic tactic and not just a philosophy. Besides, he was done with the D.C. NAACP and Reverend E. Franklin Jackson.[251]

Hobson resigned from the branch in October 1960. He had feuded with Jackson for four months over his leadership, but the last straw was the pastor's enervated response to several police brutality incidents. He decided to take action, as his role on the executive and employment committees was limited. He ran for branch secretary with several others on an anti-Jackson insurgent ticket but lost the election. Suspecting fraud, Hobson and other faction members brought charges against Jackson and the secretary and demanded their resignations in letters to the national office. The charges were dismissed, but Hobson did not leave quietly. He gave the national director of branches a piece of his mind: "I do not care who the President of the branch is, but I

DC civil rights icon Julius Hobson (*with pipe*) joined the branch in the 1950s but, disillusioned with its moderate conservative leadership, resigned in 1960. *DC Public Library.*

do care if that president is blocking the long-standing constructive work that the NAACP can do and what the DC community needs."[252]

It was for the better that Hobson and the branch parted ways. Unlike many of the city's middle to upper-class civil rights leaders, including Jackson, Hobson was a Marxist. "I believe what we're fighting over is the distribution of goods and services and the production of them; and I believe everybody…has the inalienable right to share in them," he said in an interview. That philosophy did not sit well with the branch, and Hobson was just as irritated that its leaders did not recognize capitalism as a racist and exploitative system against African Americans. Hobson's atheism further alienated him from the city's civil rights community, which was composed mostly of pastors like Jackson. His criticism of Christianity as a "haven of ministers, preachers, deacons, deaconesses, Eastern stars, and other heavenly bodies" left him without many allies.[253]

Ironically, given his apathy toward religious leaders, Hobson ushered in a new sense of direction for CORE by adopting a "selective patronage" jobs campaign organized by a coalition of four hundred Philadelphia ministers in the summer of 1960. Private companies that failed to provide equal employment opportunities to African Americans faced the wrath of Black consumer boycotts, organized by Leon Sullivan. Hobson admired this strategy and decided to blend it with traditional protest tactics of boycotts and picketing, the principal vehicle of activism utilized by the New Negro Alliance in the 1930s but rejected by the branch.[254]

The Branch versus CORE

Hobson began CORE's employment drive at Hecht's Department Store in March 1961, the same company in which Mary Church Terrell had organized lunch counter desegregation efforts a decade before. The store's Black patronage was almost 50 percent, but none of its 20 floor managers or 8 office clerks was Black. Only 5 of the 270 clerks were African American, and Black employees were limited to positions such as waitresses, stockmen, elevator operators, janitors and parking lot attendants. Hobson compiled the statistics into a memorandum and sent them to company executive Robert Levi along with a letter offering "to assist [department stores] in resulting in real merit hiring practices."[255]

Hecht's management ignored Hobson for weeks, leading him to threaten pickets and boycotts. By cleverly taking advantage of the publicity the national CORE's office garnered with the May 1961 Freedom Rides into the South to protest segregated interstate bus travel, Hobson forced Hecht's to negotiate the hiring of thirty-five Black salesclerks and one Black assistant buyer. In order to attract African American workers, the department store also agreed to include a nondiscrimination hiring clause in job announcements.[256]

Over the next nine months, CORE secured victories in Black hiring with many businesses in the city, including Hahn and Company, Mann Potato Chip Company, Wilkins Coffee Company and Warner Theaters. Landsburgh's Department Store was next. The management had promised to hire Black salesclerks in September 1958, but after four years, only seventeen of its five hundred clerical workers and supervisors were African American. In early January 1962, CORE established picket lines at all five of Landsburgh's entrances and Hobson threatened management with a citywide boycott "to make it economically necessary for you to integrate completely."[257]

The branch did not support CORE with any of these protests. "The NAACP resorts to picketing and the boycott only as a last resort," Jackson said at a press conference to calm fears that a "feud" had erupted between the two organizations. Jackson surmised that CORE's methods were too confrontational to successfully implement merit hiring. "There is no reason for the man to bargain with you if you picket," he told the *Washington Afro-*

Above: Landsburgh Department Store was one of many businesses that CORE threatened with boycotts and pickets as a means to secure equitable Black employment opportunities. The branch did not support these campaigns. *DC Public Library.*

Left: Branch president E. Franklin Jackson (*with sign*) pickets several banks on Fifteenth Street NW with several other local pastors in 1961. *DC Public Library, Star Collection © Washington Post.*

A moderate on civil rights and a fellow pastor, Reverend Walter Fauntroy (*at microphone*) of New Bethel Baptist Church in Shaw, was a perfect counterpart to Jackson. *DC Public Library, Star Collection © Washington Post.*

American. Hobson responded, "All we want Rev. Jackson to do is leave us alone for the benefit of the NAACP and the whole Washington community."[258]

The branch did leave Hobson alone. CORE forced Landsburgh's to increase its hiring of Black workers without its support, but the dispute between the two groups compelled Washington's Black clergy to take a larger role in the merit hiring program. Jackson allied himself with Reverend Walter Fauntroy, a native Washingtonian who attended Dunbar High School in the Truxton Circle neighborhood and completed his studies at Virginia Union University and Yale University's Divinity School. He returned to Washington in 1958 to become pastor at New Bethel Baptist Church in the Shaw neighborhood. In 1961, Martin Luther King Jr. tasked Fauntroy with leading the D.C. chapter of the Southern Christian Leadership Conference. With a moderate approach to civil rights like Jackson, he was a perfect counterpart. However, in late January and early February 1962, the two men pivoted. Along with thirty-five pastors from the Baptist Ministers Conference, they joined two hundred protesters in the 1300 block of F Street NW to picket against downtown merchants who refused to employ African Americans.[259]

"The Listless D.C. NAACP"

Hobson's criticism of Jackson's lethargic leadership and the branch's lack of militancy was echoed by the city's Black press. What was going on with "the listless DC NAACP" the *Washington Afro-American* inquired. The New York City, Philadelphia and Los Angeles branches agitated for fair housing laws, better jobs and equal accommodations and, most importantly, against police brutality. "But in Washington, D.C. the capital of America," the newspaper charged, "the NAACP branch has been one of the most ineffective in the country." The most egregious was its failure to condemn the southern segregationists in Congress who, as chairmen of the committees that controlled District affairs, ran the city like plantation overseers. There was a litany of men to choose from, but the *Afro* cited Senator Robert Byrd, a West Virginia Democrat and former Ku Klux Klan member who chaired a Senate appropriations subcommittee for the District, as the latest example. The branch "refused to speak out during the welfare hearings by the anti-colored Sen. Byrd" and never "once issued a statement on the possible bigotry inherent in Mr. Byrd's investigations." By contrast, the *Afro* observed, the national office had "aggressively protested an anti-black welfare plan adopted by officials in the upstate New York hamlet of Newburgh."[260]

Jackson's faults, the *Afro* said, had nothing to do with his moral character. "As a minister, a humanitarian, a political liberal—just as the fine guy he is—Rev. Jackson is one of the most outstanding men in America," it praised. He was simply "an inadequate president of the NAACP." Jackson's action—or lack thereof—raised an alarming question: "Was his silence on certain issues the result of political pressure—or even a political deal?"[261]

The *Afro* was on to something. While president, Jackson was also appointed vice chairman of the D.C. Democratic Party and was "an active member of the Democratic Central Committee for the District of Columbia (DCCDC)." In December 1962, Dolph G. Thompson, a former president of the Capital Press Club and member of the branch's executive committee, wrote to the national office, asking Roy Wilkins to investigate Jackson for prioritizing partisan activities over the branch's work. An impeachment resolution was already drafted, Thompson warned, and he urged Wilkins to expel the pastor if necessary. For the few septuagenarian and octogenarian members who remembered how John Milton Waldron's pursuit of a political appointment triggered his ouster, it was déjà vu.[262]

However, the outcome was different from 1913. Wilkins turned the issue over to Gloster B. Current, director of branches, who wrote to Thompson with finality that Jackson was in his right to serve dual roles "as long as he continues to abide by the program and policy of the Association in his activities as Branch President."[263]

Although Jackson retained the presidency, he needed to deflect lingering criticism over his DCCDC activities and focus on the branch's issues for the new year: employment, housing and discrimination in unions. They were important, but police brutality continued to be a problem, as Jackson discovered at the Northwest Community Forum at the DC Public Library's Cleveland Park branch. The new police chief was John Layton, a thirty-year veteran of the force and a former Olympic sharpshooter. Whereas Robert Murray took his orders from the District commissioners,

MPD Chief John Layton worked with white southerners on the House District of Columbia Committee to enable him to administer the department as he saw fit. *DC Public Library, Star Collection © Washington Post.*

Layton forged close relationships with southerners in Congress to let the House District Committee administer the MPD and enable him to run the department as he saw fit.[264]

On this night, Jackson and Layton clashed over various police practices. Jackson accused officers of using their firearms too often against Black citizens and engaging in "dragnet arrests" that resulted in the apprehension of any "Negro in sight." Layton denied his department's use of this method but acknowledged that it had been utilized in the past. However, the police chief did not help his argument when he emphasized that the department "can't always control the individual acts of police officers." The forum highlighted the severity of the tension between the Black community and Layton's department and the onus placed on the branch as the leading civil rights organization in the District to put an end to fatal shootings and "dragnet arrests."[265]

Jackson remained focused on police brutality and brought in another official to tackle other priorities. On January 21, 1963, he appointed Edward A. Hailes, pastor of Union Baptist Church in New Bedford, Massachusetts, as the new executive secretary. He brought a wealth of experience to Washington as a national NAACP field secretary, New Bedford NAACP

Above: Attorney General Robert Kennedy addresses participants of the 1963 "March for Freedom Now" outside the Justice Department, promising, "We can and will do better," to end discrimination in the federal government. *DC Public Library, Star Collection © Washington Post.*

Right: The branch honored NAACP field secretary Medgar Evers at its headquarters on June 14, 1963, two days after he was assassinated in Jackson, Mississippi. *DC Public Library, Star Collection © Washington Post.*

Participants of the "March for Freedom Now" listen to remarks from Reverend Smallwood Williams of the Bible Way Church in Lafayette Park. E. Franklin Jackson (beneath "SCLC Wants Freedom Now" sign) is behind Williams. *DC Public Library, Star Collection © Washington Post.*

White racist counterprotesters gathered at the Benjamin Franklin statue at Tenth Street NW and Pennsylvania Avenue during the "March for Freedom Now." *Moorland-Spingarn Research Center, Howard University.*

branch president, director of the city's Red Cross and member of the Governor's Conference on Civil Rights from 1958 to 1962. His arrival came at the right moment. In May 1963, Hobson began advocating for "open" housing laws, which would enable all Washingtonians to secure equitable housing, regardless of race. CORE's "merit hiring" campaign was also gaining more traction in the city. On June 14, 1963, the branch joined CORE and the SCLC for a "March for Freedom Now" where more than three thousand Black and white protesters marched to the District Building demanding to know "How long" Black job seekers would be treated like inferiors.[266]

The organizations were united in their support for the housing and employment initiatives, but tragedy had also brought them together. Just two days before, a single bullet from white supremacist Byron De La Beckwith's 1917 Enfield rifle mortally wounded Mississippi NAACP field secretary Medgar Evers in the driveway of his home. The crowd made its way to the Justice Department where Attorney General Robert F. Kennedy defensively answered questions about discrimination in the federal government. "We can and will do better," he promised.[267]

MARCH ON WASHINGTON FOR JOBS AND FREEDOM

Two months later, that unity fizzled. In early spring, civil rights leaders A. Philip Randolph and Bayard Rustin had planned a "March on Washington" that was primarily intended to commemorate the Emancipation Proclamation's centennial and draw attention to the unresolved issues of Black poverty and unemployment. Initially, the SCLC and several other civil rights organizations expressed disinterest. Randolph and Rustin managed to bring King, Wilkins and Andrew Young aboard, but the price they paid for their support was the downplaying of economic issues over Kennedy's civil rights legislation that had stalled in Congress.[268]

By July 1963, NAACP leaders and most of its membership supported the march, which like the 1957 Prayer Pilgrimage for Freedom would take place at the Lincoln Memorial. However, there were some dissidents. James Meredith, the first Black student to enroll at the University of Mississippi and a hero to many activists, shocked attendees at its Chicago convention when he expressed opposition. In a speech to its Youth Division banquet, Meredith rebuked "the low quality and ineffectiveness of our Negro youth leaders" and then dismissed the upcoming demonstration in Washington as an event that "would not be in the best interests of our cause." Meredith's audience remained respectful. Some wanted to boo, but did not, as he was still regarded as a martyr for his courage to integrate "Ole Miss." He received polite but tepid applause instead.[269]

Jackson was also at the convention but received no mercy. Known as a moderate within the organization, his position on the upcoming march caused him, as Malcolm Nash of the *New York Amsterdam News* reported, to be "booed so much…that he gave up his attempt to speak." Jackson infuriated many by calling for a three-day convention instead of a march. The convention also included plans for visits to Capitol Hill for lawmakers to hear activists' pleas to pass Kennedy's bill. Anger reached the boiling point when Jackson also insisted that the event be sponsored by and for NAACP members only.[270]

Jackson had yielded to fears perpetuated by the white press that a mass march on federal grounds would be unruly and violent. The *Star* questioned the validity of King's promise that "we have the machinery that will control the demonstration." Although several discussions and meetings at the convention were heated, there was no violence. Nevertheless, the *Star* churned emotions and produced a false narrative that chaos in Washington would ensue: "When it comes to controlling the actions of 100,000 or more demonstrators, there remains the distinct and dangerous possibility that he is not justified in giving such assurances."[271]

The *Afro* hit back, accusing the *Star* of trying to serve as the "great white grandfather" of a blossoming civil rights movement. A successful march would take place in the city, the newspaper promised. "The march WILL be opposed by bigots, phony white liberals, and 'Uncle Toms'," it editorialized. Jackson was one of those "Uncle Toms." His convention proposal was foolish, typical of "his thinking on civil rights," and why there was a "growing decline of respect….by the colored masses for the NAACP." It was unsurprising, the *Afro* concluded, that Black Washingtonians were "turning to SCLC, CORE, and SNCC."[272]

Jackson abandoned his convention plans, but the branch still played a dominant role in the march's planning. Hailes and Fauntroy co-chaired the Washington Coordinating Committee, a coalition of pastors and presidents of local civil rights organizations, to organize District residents and ensure the safety of the marchers. Other members included Belford Lawson (DC Mobilization Committee), Sterling Tucker (Washington Urban League), Bishop Smallwood Williams (SCLC), E. Charles Brown (Howard University's student Nonviolent Action Group) and Hobson. Committee

Planning meetings for the March on Washington for Jobs and Freedom were held at the branch's headquarters at 1417 U Street NW. *DC Public Library, Star Collection © Washington Post.*

meetings were held at the branch's headquarters at 1417 U Street NW. The tasks were challenging: strategies to mobilize local residents to attend, ways to coordinate with law enforcement to maintain order and the means of ensuring an "early in, early out" plan that would require demonstrators to be on the grounds at sunrise and depart by 5:00 p.m.[273]

Low turnout by Washingtonians was a major concern for the branch. The viability of the movement would certainly be questioned by critics if a small percentage of the majority-Black city's residents attended. Organizers hoped to recruit forty to fifty thousand Washingtonians. On August 6, 1963, Tucker told committee members: "There may be a tendency for local people to stay home. They may think this is somebody else's march. But this is everybody's march." It was imperative for the branch that there would be no repeat of the sparse attendance that had scarred the Prayer Pilgrimage.[274]

The branch sponsored a rally on August 25 at Howard University's William H. Greene Stadium as a final pitch to energize Washingtonians for the march. Jackson spoke to a packed crowd of three thousand, but

Left: Myrlie Evers, widow of Medgar Evers, addressed an NAACP rally at Howard University on August 25, 1963, three days before the March on Washington. *DC Public Library, Star Collection © Washington Post.*

Opposite: Aerial view of crowds at the Lincoln Memorial during the March on Washington. *DC Public Library*

everyone really came to see and hear Medgar Evers' widow, Myrlie. Those in attendance, Evers said, were soldiers just like her husband who "was found dying on a southern battlefield—this particular battlefield was Jackson, Mississippi." She urged everyone to take up his cause, but to do it "with love, determination, and courage," and received a long standing ovation when she closed by quoting the end of the Gettysburg Address.[275]

The rally's purpose was twofold. Medgar Evers had worked tirelessly for the NAACP in the most racist state in America. The branch had honored him on the same day of the June 14 freedom march with CORE and the SCLC but wanted to continue paying homage. However, Jackson also used the event—which included no speakers from other civil rights groups—to demonstrate that the NAACP was still the most relevant and viable organization in the District. Evers's appearance had definitely rallied the faithful, but Jackson also hoped it would confirm that message.

Roughly 250,000 demonstrators congregated at the Lincoln Memorial on August 28, 1963, including 40,000 to 50,000 Washingtonians, far exceeding the 100,000 that officials expected. The coordination between volunteers, municipal and federal officials, transportation planners and law enforcement resulted in a successful event with no disruptions or security issues. The American Nazi Party, headquartered in Arlington, Virginia, attempted to disrupt the march after its founder, George Lincoln Rockwell, failed to get Governor Albertis S. Harrison to condemn the event and endorse his cause. Rockwell was one of the most vocal proponents of white supremacy and the segregationist status quo during the 1960s and was an unsuccessful candidate in the 1964 Virginia gubernatorial race before his assassination three years later by a former ANP member. Although boastful in his special August 1963 *Rockwell Report* and in a letter to Harrison that "tens of thousands of fighting White men…will do everything to smash the black revolution on August 28," Rockwell's mission failed miserably. Only 74 members showed up at the Washington Monument for a rally at 6:00 a.m., where 200 Washington police officers and National Guard MIPs awaited. Five hours later, ANP deputy commander Karl Rogers Allen was arrested for speaking without a permit, and the group "then trailed off single file across [the] 14th St. Bridge…[and] returned quietly to their Arlington headquarters." Perturbed that his army never materialized, Rockwell criticized "the cowardice of the white race."[276]

Crowd at the March on Washington. *DC Public Library.*

Seeking relief from the heat, an NAACP marcher drinks from a water truck fountain. *DC Public Library.*

Washingtonians were not monolithic in their assessment of the march. Most believed it was a monumental step toward freedom and equality, but just as many thought it was an empty spectacle of theatrics that ignored issues unique to the District. The lack of home rule was a glaring example. The criticism from Black power advocates and other non-accommodationist voices was particularly stark, especially since some had participated in the march's operational logistics. As the coordinator of an auxiliary force of more than five hundred marshals who assisted police with maintaining order and crowd control, Hobson witnessed firsthand King's electrifying "I Have a Dream" address and young SNCC chairman John Lewis's denunciation of Kennedy's civil rights bill. Nevertheless, he dismissed the event as just "a bunch of emotional speeches." Malcolm X, the national spokesman for the Nation of Islam (NOI), who had rallied ten thousand supporters at the Uline Arena in Northeast Washington in 1961 and served briefly as interim minister of Mosque #4 on New Jersey Avenue in 1963, sarcastically referred to it as the "Farce on Washington" whose sole purpose was "to keep the Negroes from getting too far out of line."[277]

Sondra B. Hassan, a native Washingtonian who accompanied Malcolm X to the March as a member of SNCC, could have done without all the speeches too. "We in SNCC had another idea of how this March was going to go," she said in a 2013 interview. "We were going to shut down the city [and] lay bodies on the bridges….Well, we got talked out of all that." These statements underscored the jousting philosophies of Washington's fragmented civil rights leadership. The march was the last significant event that embodied a semblance of unity between the branch and other groups in the city.[278]

H. Carl Moultrie Becomes Branch President

By 1964, organizational changes had dramatically altered local Washington's civil rights leadership. The *Afro*'s hunch about Jackson's political aspirations were correct. In January, the pastor resigned from the branch to seek the post of Democratic National committeeman. He was succeeded by first vice president H. Carl Moultrie, a former journalist, social worker and housing official from Wilmington, North Carolina, who came to Washington in 1948 as the national executive secretary of Omega Psi Phi, a noted Black fraternity.[279]

H. Carl Moultrie served as branch president from 1964 to 1968. *DC Public Library.*

Meanwhile, Hobson became frustrated with CORE. Much to his chagrin, the organization was overly focused on the philosophy of nonviolence. At the same time, Hobson's aggressive personality irritated members. Protests had brought about "token changes," he concluded, and now only "political and economic power will bring about permanent change." In June 1964, one month before President Johnson signed the Civil Rights Act, a rebellious faction ousted Hobson from the D.C. chapter. Angered but still determined, he formed the Association of Community Teams (ACT), a new militant organization that made clear that if white people wanted to participate, they would have to seek another group. The rejection of white membership was not out of hate, one internal memo insisted: "WE JUST DON'T NEED THEM." The ACT also indicated it would not support conservative Black interests. One of its main objectives—"isolate Uncle Tom"—was certainly a criticism directed at the branch.[280]

Through the ACT, Hobson engaged in activities in the city ("guerilla tactics" and "psychological welfare" as he called them) that contrasted sharply with the protest tactics of the branch. For example, he captured rats scampering about in poor neighborhoods, placed them in cages attached to his car's roof and threatened to release them into Georgetown if city officials continued to ignore rodent infestations in the District's Black neighborhoods. These "Rat Relocation Rallies" were a publicity stunt. Hobson never released any into the white, affluent enclave; he simply drowned them at night. However, the move forced city leaders to adopt an extermination program in Northwest D.C.[281]

Hobson's "Rat Wagon" also doubled as the "Cop Watching Wagon" in which he would tail police cruisers and yell to officers through a loudspeaker, demanding they treat citizens with professionalism and respect. Branch leaders never considered such measures to address poor neighborhood conditions or police-community relations. While Hobson engaged in these confrontations in the city, Hailes met with white conservatives in Glen Burnie, Maryland, to discourage them from forming White Citizens Councils in the Maryland and Virginia suburbs outside the District. It was a noble cause but, at the same time, exemplified what Washington journalist Hayes Johnson described as a growing rift between the Black working class and the poor and the "old-line, well-established" organizations like the branch. Its traditional lobbying, petitions and other nonconfrontational methods had become tiresome and ineffective. Many Black Washingtonians simply felt alienated from the leadership that Moultrie and Hailes championed. They wanted agitators, radicals and troublemakers.[282]

MARION BARRY AND THE 1966 D.C. BUS BOYCOTT

Marion Barry noticed the disconnect when he arrived in Washington in June 1965. Born in Itta Bena, Mississippi, Barry's activism took an early start when he joined the local NAACP chapter while pursuing a master's degree in organic chemistry at the historically Black Fisk University. He joined lunch counter sit-in demonstrations in Nashville after four students from North Carolina A&T University attempted to integrate a Woolworth's lunch counter in Greensboro. In April 1960, Barry became the first chairman of SNCC, and by May 1965, executive secretary James Forman had dispatched Barry to Washington to lobby Congress on civil rights legislation and fill the organization's coffers to finance operations in the South.[283]

Barry became impatient with SNCC fundraising projects and soon engaged the Black community in local organizing initiatives. In the mid-1960s, the capital's transportation system was limited to cars and buses. In 1962, Washington eliminated electric streetcars, and the Metrorail subway system would not open for another decade. The bus system was operated by a single company, DC Transit, and owned by O. Roy Chalk, a wealthy real estate mogul and owner of a small Caribbean airline. In September 1965, Chalk imposed a 25 percent fare increase that was rejected by community organizations, churches and civil rights activists as unfair to lower-income workers who comprised a majority of the bus-riding population.[284]

SNCC mobilized community opposition. On November 7, 1965, it hosted a rally at Shiloh Baptist Church where the branch and ACT called for a boycott against DC Transit. On December 28, Barry announced a one-day boycott on January 24, 1966, to demonstrate "that the Washington area public is united in opposition to the fare increase."[285]

The branch's call for the boycott had more to do with the hope of avoiding criticism from SNCC, ACT and the Black community and less to do with

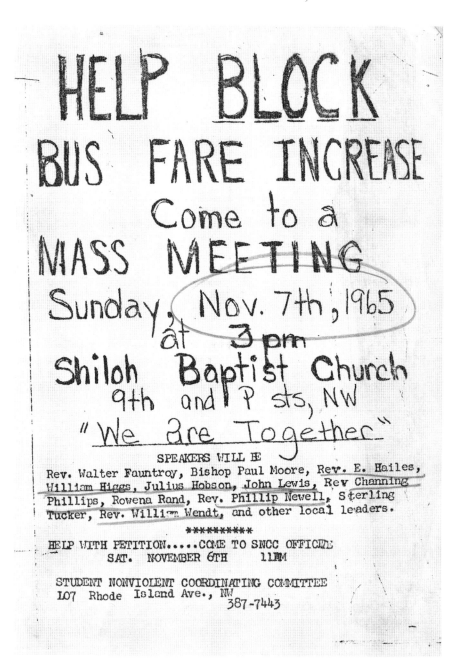

Civil rights leaders mobilized community opposition to the bus fare increase with a rally at Shiloh Baptist Church on November 7, 1965. The branch endorsed the boycott but offered no support. *DC Public Library.*

condemning Chalk and the impact of the fare increase on passengers. Its support did not extend beyond the endorsement. SNCC and ACT adopted a more active role in community mobilization. Members printed and distributed over 175,000 flyers, and SNCC workers operated three sound trucks that roved through Black neighborhoods to spread the word. It paid off. Over 75,000 people refused to ride the buses on that frigid day, which resulted in the loss of an estimated 150,000 fares for DC Transit. Two days later, the Metropolitan Area Transit Commission voted to reject the fare increase. MATC director Delmer Ison attributed the rejection to accounting and cost issues, and the *Star* editorialized that the boycott had no role. Declaring victory, Barry knew the truth. And so did Black Washingtonians.[286]

The boycott's success emboldened Barry to focus next on the issue in which organizations in Washington had produced no tangible results for decades: home rule. Despite calls for its passage as early as 1949, the branch's priority was segregation, not self-government. The Washington Home Rule Committee, an interracial group established in the 1940s, was largely ineffective. It also did not help that local leaders did not address it at the March on Washington. That criticism was a sore spot for King, who by 1965 was deeply concerned about the District's local political structure, particularly the power wielded by southern segregationists like McMillan and Byrd, who headed the House and Senate District Committees, respectively.[287]

The Branch and the Free D.C. Movement

In August, King returned to the capital in support of President Johnson's proposed home rule bill that would provide an elected mayor and city council. Unlike in August 1963, he rallied five thousand Washingtonians directly in a two-day swing through the city as a community organizer. It was an exhaustive whirlwind tour with eight appearances, including street corner rallies at Ninth Street and Rhode Island Avenue NW; First and L Streets NW; Fourteenth Street and Park Road NW; and a park in Deanwood, a neighborhood in Northeast. The crowds expressed excitement, with signs proclaiming "King Is Great," freedom songs and chants of his name. At each stop, he offered them a fiery promise: "Home rule is so basic that if it is not soon passed by Congress, there may be some mass demonstrations." King ended that first day with an 8:00 p.m. gathering at Metropolitan Baptist Church, where he had huddled with branch leaders eight years earlier to finalize plans for the Prayer Pilgrimage for Freedom.[288]

King's appeal to Washingtonians did not extend to Congress. Along with the DC Coalition of Conscience—a network of forty civic, religious and civil rights groups, chaired by Fauntroy and Paul Moore, a white, Episcopal bishop—King concluded his visit with a vigil in Lafayette Park to garner support for home rule. However, as he had done since 1949 when he took control of the House District Committee, McMillan led lawmakers' successful actions to vote down the legislation.[289]

Despite this setback, Barry seized the initiative by announcing a campaign to "Free D.C." From whom? Surrounded by local clergy, Barry identified those enemies at a February 24, 1966 press conference: "We want to free D.C. from…the people who make it impossible for us to do anything about lousy schools, brutal cops, slumlords, welfare investigators…employers who discriminate in hiring and a host of other ills." The terminology was deliberate, Barry told the *Post*. The people "want to vote," he insisted. "They just don't respond to the name 'home rule.'"[290]

The branch initially supported the Free DC movement, which targeted downtown businesses owned by members of the Washington Board of Trade, an opponent of home rule for years. A door-to-door campaign began with activists asking store owners to place orange and black Free DC stickers in their windows and contribute money for a national advertising campaign to promote self-government in the District. However, the support was short-lived. Free DC volunteers targeted white merchants in the predominantly Black commercial districts of the H Street corridor to support the home rule petitions. Exerting pressure on the stubborn holdouts, Barry threatened an economic boycott against those proprietors on March 5, 1966. Just as Jackson had denounced the CORE boycotts, Hailes announced his opposition to Barry's plan, arguing that the strategy amounted to extortion and blackmail and that no business should be punished economically because it did not subscribe to another's political convictions. "A person has a right to dissent," he said. Six days later, the branch's executive board voted unanimously to withdraw its endorsement of the movement after Hailes declared that the boycott's objectives "are not clearly defined."[291]

Barry offered mild criticism of the decision. As a member of the Coalition of Conscience, the branch was a constituent of Free DC, so its withdrawal, Barry said, "did not help much." He left it at that, but African American journalists were exasperated, especially after branch officials further complicated their position with mixed messaging. Several days after Hailes's announcement, Moultrie appeared at a news conference and expressed his support "as an individual." He startled reporters by declaring

Right: Marion Barry discusses the Free DC movement with reporters at the District Building in 1966. *DC Public Library, Star Collection © Washington Post.*

Below: A father and son march along H Street NE on March 12, 1966, in support of the Free DC movement. The branch withdrew its support after a change in strategy included economic boycotts. *DC Public Library, Star Collection © Washington Post.*

"the NAACP never said it was not in support of the boycott plan." Hailes responded that Moultrie probably meant that he regarded the boycott "as a legitimate tool under certain circumstances." The contradictory statements rankled the *Post*'s William Raspberry, who wrote that Black Washingtonians were not being well served by the branch's "puzzling" policy. The two men obviously did not want to lose their identification with the "grassroots" people the Free DC movement was trying to involve, the columnist said, but at the same time, they had misgivings about backing a program that they deemed morally and technically unsound. Nevertheless, Raspberry wrote, the branch owed it to the people to be boldly courageous and take a stand one way or the other. Black Washingtonians had no appetite for waffling.[292]

The Free DC movement was ultimately unsuccessful, as a unified local and federal white establishment presented insurmountable challenges for Black activists to achieve home rule. However, these forces targeted Barry, and not the branch, which had also supported Free DC, albeit briefly. The *Post* dismissed the movement as a "free-swinging band of home rule militants." The Washington Board of Trade and the Federation of Citizens Associations, a coalition of white neighborhood groups, played on white Washingtonians' fears of the Black empowerment that Barry's activism could bring to the city. "They can do it for the Democrats or for the XYZ welfare program or any cause they choose to back," an open letter to the public ominously warned. McMillan initiated an investigation of Barry for allegedly violating a federal anti-racketeering law and dismissed Free DC as "a Communist plot." He also prevented legislation from receiving a House floor vote, effectively killing home rule for the District. These opponents, which the branch had fought for years as the dominant civil rights organization in Washington, did not include it in their condemnation of Free DC. They did not need to. The branch had become irrelevant to them.[293]

"BLACK POWER: GOOD OR BAD?"

By the fall of 1966, Black Power radicals vigorously appealed to branch leaders to adopt and embrace this new brand of activism. In September, Barry and Jefferson P. Rogers, pastor of the Church of the Redeemer, dominated a "Black Power: Good or Bad?" discussion at a branch meeting at Lincoln Temple. The Free DC campaign had been all about Black

Power, Barry told the one hundred seated members. Organizing around one's Blackness, Barry argued, was the "thrust to relieve oppression." For Rogers, African Americans needed to embrace their role as a "potential disrupter" to achieve control. "The Negro is no longer satisfied just to stay alive," he preached.[294]

An October 1966 *Washington Post* article that surveyed "a cross-section" of Black Washingtonians offered hope to both the branch and Black Power advocates. "The mood of the Negro in Washington is optimistic for the future—but tough and militant for the present," it began. It found that four out of five Black Washingtonians professed a belief in nonviolence, "but at the same time, the trend seems to be for more militant tactics in the push for civil rights."[295]

The path toward militancy was favorable for Hobson and Barry, but the article also contained a poll that was good news for the branch. Residents were asked whether they thought various organizations were helpful or hurtful to civil rights causes and compared them to national figures. The NAACP, SCLC, CORE, SNCC and National Urban League were more popular in Washington than the rest of the country, but the NAACP ranked the highest in the city with 87 percent approval. Some groups trailed closely behind: SCLC (74 percent), Urban League (67 percent) and CORE (62 percent), while the others fared worse: SNCC (43 percent), Coalition of Conscience (34 percent), ACT (26 percent) and Black Muslims (9 percent).[296]

The poll's findings were attributed to the population's familiarity with the NAACP as the nation's eldest civil rights organization. Although the study was based on the groups' national identities, the branch was emboldened to advocate the NAACP as the sole organization that could alleviate the hardships that African Americans in Washington faced. Violent crime, which surged in the District in the 1960s, was a primary issue, as was police brutality. Aggressive complaints against racist officers in the Metropolitan Police Department and several victories in high-profile cases in 1965–66 convinced Moultrie that the branch would prevail."[297]

The Ku Klux Klan apparently believed it too. One week after the *Post* analysis, Hailes found a handwritten sign posted on the branch's front door. "Knights of the KKK. We Are Watching You," it ominously read. That was good news, Hailes told reporters, after notifying the MPD and FBI. It meant that these white supremacists feared the organization and its work.[298]

"The Washington Branch of the NAACP Is Broke"

What a difference a year made though. By November 1967, the branch was in shambles financially, organizationally and spiritually. "We're broke," Hailes announced at a press conference shortly before he resigned to take a job with the Washington Institute for Employment Training, an anti-poverty agency. "You can tell the public that. The Washington branch of the NAACP is broke." Hailes had secured fifteen thousand members the previous year, but now that number was less than half. Normal daily office tasks were difficult. Mary Alice Jervay, the lone secretary, worked hard to answer calls while also trying to get out mailings on a mimeograph machine that was seldom functional. Even conditions in the surrounding neighborhood increased anxieties. The office was locked with three deadbolts after a rash of break-ins lost the branch two typewriters. Two doors down at 1421 U Street, jewelry store owner Louise Mosby was killed during an attempted robbery of her business. "Drunks come in off the street," an impatient Jervay once told a visitor who could not fathom the necessity for the locked door.[299]

The branch's financial troubles were due in part to a bylaw provision mandating that the national office collect half of all funds raised by the organization's chapters. However, the drop in membership was self-inflicted. That summer, tensions over aggressive policing, poor housing and unemployment culminated in destructive riots throughout the country. The worst were in Newark, New Jersey, and Detroit, Michigan, which resulted in a total of sixty-nine people killed, 8,600 arrests and $50 million in property damage. That widespread violence did not erupt in Washington, but Black community–white police relations were similar to the conditions that sparked the bedlam in these other urban centers.[300]

The branch's 1957 police brutality and discrimination suit revealed only 11 percent of the department was African American. By 1967, that number had grown only to 20 percent. The *Wall Street Journal* reported that Black residents viewed the District's police force as nothing more than an "army of occupation" and "full of racist cops who hate Negroes." The branch's response did not ameliorate the problem. Calling for "respect for law and order," Moultrie urged citizens not to protest police arrests and brutality but to simply file formal complaints with the branch. His constant drumbeats that "the policeman is here to protect all citizens" and that peaceful demonstrations always eventually led to "mob violence" went unheard and angered Black Washingtonians. The police were disrespecting and brutalizing them. They would not be lectured to about the importance of respecting law and order.[301]

The branch replaced Hailes with Dudley Williams, a twenty-eight-year-old Howard Law School graduate and attorney from Martinsville, Virginia. At his announcement press conference, he took a subtle swing at Black Power radicals by praising the legacy of the NAACP—the organization that stood for "orderly process and emphasis on court action." After dodging questions about what specific issues the branch would address, Moultrie seized the microphone and declared the focus would be on discrimination in the media and the federal and District governments, but was just as vague on details. However, Williams was unflinchingly direct on one probing question. Vowing to engage with "all civil rights organizations," he was asked if that included Black militants. It did not.[302]

THE BRANCH AND THE BLACK UNITED FRONT

In January 1968, Stokely Carmichael, the most ardent Black Power advocate, decided the time for action was now. A slender Bronxite with Trinidadian roots, Carmichael got his start in activism in the Nonviolent Action Group (NAG), an alliance of Howard University students to combat racism and segregation in the capital. "On Howard's campus, we were a solid, highly visible community unified by…a conviction that youth could change the world," he once recalled. However, Carmichael found himself spending more time fighting Jim Crow in the South, mobilizing voter registration drives and being incarcerated for it all. As one of the first to captivate supporters for "Black Power!" in a 1966 speech in the Mississippi Delta, he became SNCC chairman that same year after the organization renounced and expelled its white membership.[303]

Washington was the ideal place for Carmichael's operational base. Seeking for activists to speak with one voice "for a rightful and proportionate share in the decision making councils of the District, and rightful and proportionate control of economic institutions in the Black community," Carmichael organized the Black United Front (BUF), a coalition of moderate and progressive groups, at the New School for Afro-American Thought, a cultural center on Fourteenth Street.[304]

Reporters shivered in the frigid cold outside the building, curious about the participants. Who were the people who decided to attend this conference? Why would they want to come out for this Stokely Carmichael, who, as

Black United Front member C. Sumner Stone addresses fellow members at a July 1968 meeting as *(from left)* Reverend Walter Fauntroy, Stokely Carmichael and Tony Cox listen. The branch refused to join the BUF. *DC Public Library, Star Collection © Washington Post.*

white WTOP radio host Jack Jurey charged, had a "well-deserved reputation for acute extremism"? There were many attendees, but some were motivated only by their own self-interest. "Everyone showed up because nobody could afford not to be recognized as a black leader," recalled C. Sumner "Chuck" Stone, a former *Washington Afro American* editor and chief administrative aide to Representative Adam Clayton Powell Jr., who sat on the BUF Board of Directors. Moultrie attended but, along with other moderate-conservative organizations like the Washington Urban League and Committee of 100 Ministers, ultimately declined to join the BUF.[305]

Some of the branch's lack of participation in the BUF was attributed to its past clashes with the national office. NAACP executive secretary Roy Wilkins, who had a conservatively practical outlook and approach to civil rights, was vehemently opposed to Black militancy and Carmichael in particular. He instructed the national board of directors to pressure Moultrie to not affiliate with the SNCC leader under any circumstances. Moultrie, in no mood for yet another raucous feud with the New York headquarters, complied.[306]

However, even if the national NAACP had never issued an ultimatum to the branch, militant BUF members were apprehensive about the organization and questioned Moultrie's intentions from the beginning. Echoing William Calvin Chase's criticisms that the NAACP was a white-controlled organization, BUF member Reginald Booker asserted that branch rank-and-file were untrustworthy. They came to the conference only because "the white man through his propaganda machine began to ask questions of how could these so-called established Negroes sit in a room with Stokely Carmichael."[307]

Branch Supports a "Poor People's Campaign"

In early spring 1968, Moultrie signaled his intent to finally adopt the confrontational protest tactics that Hobson, Barry and others had long advocated. This change was attributed to King, who had evolved from a focus on racism and white supremacy in the South to a broader critique of war, capitalism and poverty. He planned a Poor People's Campaign to bring attention to poverty not just in Washington, but the entire nation. Moderation and lack of confrontation had been a key element of the 1963 march, but 1968 was going to be different. King threatened to "tie up transportation in Washington, jam the hospitals, boycott the schools, and sit-in at Government offices."[308]

It was inevitable that King would plan such a demonstration in the capital. He hinted his intentions as early as December 1956 with his "Remember Who You Are?" sermon at Howard University: "I'm concerned about the tragic gulf between superfluous inordinate wealth and abject poverty. I'm not only concerned about mansions over yonder…but…about the slums in this city." King gave two more high-profile addresses in Washington devoted to the campaign in February and March 1968. On February 8, he held a two-hour meeting with Carmichael and SNCC leader H. Rap Brown at the Pitts Motel, 1451 Belmont Street NW to discuss goals and logistics. The motel became a landmark in the history of 1968 activism as an official headquarters of the PPC that housed many of its planners. The meeting ran late, but a crowd of more than six hundred, including branch members, waited patiently at Vermont Avenue Baptist Church to hear King outline his vision. His "In Search of a Sense of Direction" sermon was an indictment of the Johnson administration's shift away from the plight of the poor in America and a focus "in Vietnam." He boldly promised, "When we come here…we will come to demand that the nation grant us what is truly ours."[309]

For those who still questioned the importance of the demonstration, King's sermon ("Remaining Awake Through a Great Revolution") at the National Cathedral on Wisconsin Avenue provided a sharper vision than his previous appearances. Standing at the ornate podium high above the three thousand parishioners, King assured his audience that "we are not coming to tear up Washington" but also insisted it was a revolution for "the tired, the poor [and] the huddled masses" to finally gain the unalienable rights enshrined in the Declaration of Independence. "If a man doesn't have a job or income, he has neither life nor liberty nor the possibility for the pursuit of happiness. He merely exists."[310]

Wilkins was incensed that King included Carmichael and Brown in the PPC's preparation, but he should not have been surprised. As early as 1966, King had spent time mending the splintering factions of civil rights groups, and Black militants were no exception. An early and frequent critic of the "Black Power!" slogan, King reaffirmed his allegiance to nonviolence but did not sign a manifesto drafted by civil rights leaders in Atlanta that year that condemned Black radicals. As the SCLC leader finalized plans, Wilkins charged in a National Press Club speech that King would not be able to control the crowds that these militants would bring to the city to wreak havoc. Important civil rights legislation was on the brink of passage, Wilkins said, and their presence would definitely "ruffle the feathers" of lawmakers and the Johnson administration. "The trouble with the black militants is that they preach the very thing that has brought them to their unhappy state—racism." If King had no problem being manipulated by Carmichael and Brown, then he was on his own, Wilkins said. The NAACP would not support the PPC.[311]

The branch decided it would. Dismissing national treasurer Alfred Lewis's accusation that King was practicing "his own peculiar kind of brinkmanship" and that the march was "a dangerous thing," Moultrie broke from the headquarters in the most autonomous clash between the two units since the 1937–39 dispute. "I run the Washington office of the NAACP and I will decide what makes good sense for Washington," Moultrie said. Concerns about the influence of Black militants were trivial compared to the importance of jobs. If groups advocated for businesses and teachers in Congress, Moultrie reasoned, then it was just as appropriate for those with no job or income to do the same. "It is right that the poor come to Washington to lobby for their needs," he announced at the branch's 1968 membership drive.[312]

APRIL 4, 1968, AND THE UPRISING IN D.C.

Yvonne Baskerville, a Dunbar High School graduate and Census Bureau employee, thought she was going to have a stroke when she was driving on Fourteenth Street and heard radio announcer "Nighthawk Terry" report that King had been shot at the Lorraine Motel in Memphis, Tennessee. "I mean I was just devastated." The official news of King's death came at 8:19 p.m. By then, crowds near the branch and SNCC offices at Fourteenth and U and W Streets, respectively, were more than just devastated. They were ready for revenge. "The shit is going to hit the fan now. Let's get some white motherfuckers," someone said. "Let's kill them all," threatened another.[313]

Carmichael, who viewed King as a mentor, was able to quell the outbreak of violence at first. He and other SNCC members walked down Fourteenth Street and asked businesses to close out of respect for the slain King. They complied. The first to close were Eaton's Barber Shop, Yankee Restaurant and Wings 'N' Things. But around 9:30 p.m., a window of the People's Drug Store, where Eugene Davidson had led New Negro Alliance protests, was smashed. And so the rioting and vandalizing began. Looters broke into Sam's Pawnbrokers and Rhodes Five-and-Ten and incinerated a car at the Barry-Pate-Addison Chevrolet. Police battled rioters, and firefighters were pelted with stones when they arrived to extinguish the many blazes that had been set. A soaking rain finally stopped the mayhem that first night, but not before Black neighborhoods all over the city, including the Seventh Street NW and H Street NE areas, were affected.[314]

Washington was fairly quiet the next morning, but by the afternoon, the rioting had resumed. Areas that had been struck the previous night were targeted again. Quality Clothing, one of the numerous jewelry stores, hardware shops, liquor franchises, pawnshops and salons hit, was looted before teenagers started a fire inside the building. As police officers released tear gas on the crowds and firefighters raced around the city, Leyton reported an undeniable reality to his boss, Public Safety Director Patrick Murphy: the MPD could no longer control the uprising. It was time for a federal response.[315]

At 4:00 p.m., less than twenty-four hours after King's assassination, President Johnson deployed federal troops to restore order. At 5:30 p.m., Mayor Walter Washington declared a state of emergency. Alcohol, gasoline containers and firearms were banned, and a curfew was imposed until 6:30 a.m. Saturday, April 6. Significant sections of the city lay in ruins when the 13,450 National Guard soldiers began to leave on April 10.[316]

A Howard University student expresses her reaction to the assassination of Martin Luther King Jr. at a campus vigil service on April 5, 1968. *DC Public Library, Star Collection © Washington Post.*

A police officer stands in front of a damaged storefront at People's Drugs Store during the uprising. *DC Public Library, Star Collection © Washington Post.*

King's assassination angered and saddened many District civil rights leaders, including Moultrie. "It's the most tragic thing that we've had happen in this nation for a long time." As a member of the Mayor's Urban Coalition—a federation of civic, business and religious organizations established "to develop action programs in the private and public sectors of the area"—Moultrie met with Washington and other local officials during the uprising at the District Building to monitor the situation. He also toured the damaged Fourteenth and U and V Streets area with the mayor each day and night. That close relationship paid off. Without hesitation, Washington appointed Moultrie chair of the Coalition's Emergency Employment Committee and also placed him on its housing committee, chaired by Sterling Tucker. Moultrie now had the necessary resources from the city to coordinate an employment drive for the estimated 2,500 now out of work. The branch also now had the clout to project the image that it was the sole organization dedicated to bringing some semblance of comfort and aid to traumatized Black Washingtonians. At least that is what Moultrie hoped.[317]

Mayor Walter Washington (*center*) at the intersection of Fourteenth and V Streets with Acting Police Chief Jerry Wilson (*left*) during the DC uprising. H. Carl Moultrie joined the mayor on some of these tours. *DC Public Library, Star Collection © Washington Post.*

He got to work immediately. While the Council of Churches of Greater Washington, Catholic Archdiocese of Washington and Jewish Community Council coordinated more than thirty food distribution centers, Moultrie established five job placement offices at 3308 Fourteenth Street NW, 1000 U Street NW, 516 H Street NE, 1331 Savannah Street NE and 515 Eighth Street SE and an employment center at the branch office.[318]

Through working the phones and assisting walk-ins for twenty-four hours, volunteers and branch board members received 417 offers from local businesses for $1.60-per-hour jobs, which exceeded the 303 that came in to the other five locations combined. More than six hundred Black applicants had been reached. The numbers were impressive, but Executive Secretary Williams was still displeased. The branch had connected with Black residents just as much as it had not. Many received the help they solicited, but Williams noted that very few volunteered to help with the drive. "Most…with the exception of the board members, were white," a frustrated Williams said in a *Post* interview.[319]

There was a reason for that. In late April, Moultrie underscored the importance of preserving King's legacy by spearheading a drive to rename landmarks in the Washington metropolitan area. Armed with petitions, branch members canvassed the city to rename downtown K Street "Martin Luther King Street" and construct a memorial park somewhere in "the west end." Across the Potomac River in Virginia, National Airport was to be renamed after the fallen civil rights leader. Despite these commendable actions, Moultrie's reasoning for the uprising illustrated the branch's disconnect to the Black community. Others had spoken directly to its anger. "You just can't expect people not to react this way," said Edward J. Maclane, president of the Federation of Civic Associations, of the violence. "The city has been heading this way for a long time." Whether or not he intended to be taken literally, Hobson was more blunt: "I say that the next white man who comes into the black community preaching non-violence should be dealt with violently." Militant SNCC leader Lester J. McKinnie attributed King's assassination to "the white racist government of the United States" and was an example of "what is in store for all of us—the African people in America." By comparison, Moultrie attributed the uprising to congressional leaders' "refusal to pass the gun control and crime bills."[320]

END OF A DECADE

Organizers proceeded with King's Poor People's Campaign in May 1968, but it ultimately failed to secure federal anti-poverty legislation. Due to the local SCLC's dominance, the branch played no significant role in the demonstration except to locate housing for marchers after the dismantling of the Resurrection City encampment. The organization continued to decline in early fall of 1968. Bruce Dunkins, who coordinated its annual Freedom Fund Ball at the Sheraton Park Hotel, believed its resurrection was dependent on blockbuster fundraisers and sold-out Miss NAACP beauty contests. Black militants and white racists or "the burners and haters," as Dunkins called them, were "getting all the attention" and responsible for the branch's problems. The philosophy of moderation and the uplifting message of racial solidarity were the only viable solutions for Black empowerment in the District. "I sincerely feel that most people, Negro and white, prefer our way of doing things," Dunkins argued.[321]

Others felt differently. Williams finally acknowledged what Black Washingtonians had conveyed to the branch in the 1960s: it had an image problem. The association had always been a legal-oriented organization, but

Organizers proceeded with King's Poor People's Campaign in May 1968, but the demonstration fell short of its goal to secure federal anti-poverty legislation. *DC Public Library.*

the challenges now facing residents required a new strategy. "You have to be socially and economically in the black community today," Williams said.[322]

Leading the branch through a period of strife and crisis in the District had been exhausting for Moultrie. In November 1968, he did not seek reelection. In December, 1,031 members cast ballots in an all-day election, turning to Edward Hailes, a familiar face, to succeed Moultrie. The new board members were some of the youngest the branch ever had, but Hailes was experienced and seasoned, returning after spending two additional years working on jobs and poverty issues. Upon accepting the presidency, Hailes pledged the branch would be the most active of the 2,000 in the country. The 1960s had proven that would be no easy task. He had a lot of work to do.[323]

CONCLUSION

Almost six decades after William Calvin Chase predicted that the NAACP would not thrive in the District, his argument had validity. His rejection of the branch as a body controlled by white people and out of touch with the capital's African American residents in 1910 were echoed by Black radicals in the 1960s. Although it was responsible for the dismantling of legal segregation in restaurants, housing, schools, transportation systems and recreation spaces from the 1910s to the 1950s, it failed to adequately address the issues of racial, political and economic inequality that emerged in the 1960s.

The 1970s ushered in significant changes to the political landscape in Washington as federal powerbrokers heeded residents' demands to be treated as first-class citizens. In 1970, Congress passed and President Richard Nixon signed a bill establishing the office of nonvoting delegate in Congress. Washingtonians were not granted a vote, as the office had no power, but it was still a victory in the fight for full representation on Capitol Hill. Black nationalists and white liberals vowed to make the District the fifty-first state and formed the DC Statehood Committee to accomplish that goal. In 1971, Hobson engaged in a bitter campaign against Fauntroy as the candidate of the new DC Statehood Party. In 1972, African American voters in McMillan's South Carolina district finally toppled the segregationist, paving the way for home rule. In December 1973, Congress passed the DC Home Rule Act, which created a mayor elected by the people as well as a thirteen-member council.[324]

As much as the branch was connected to these events, it declined in Washington during this time, as African Americans demanded changes through electoral participation rather than traditional civil rights activism. Whereas leaders like Hobson and Barry had been crusading forces in the NAACP, they now believed that Black Washingtonians could be better

Local preparatory school students show their support for home rule at the District Building during a 1973 rally. *DC Public Library, Star Collection © Washington Post.*

Mayor Walter Washington speaking to the crowd at the District Building during the 1973 home rule rally. *DC Public Library, Star Collection © Washington Post.*

served on the city council (Hobson in 1974) and in the office of the mayor (Barry in 1978).

As of this writing, post-1970 records of the District of Columbia branch of the NAACP were not available. Accessibility and further examination of these records is not only necessary but also vital in order to fully document the rich history and legacy of this organization, which continues to fight on behalf of all Washingtonians today.

NOTES

Introduction

1. "Brief Services For Mrs. Terrell in Washington," *Baltimore Afro-American* [hereafter *BAA*], August 7, 1954; "Mary Church Terrell," *Washington Evening Star* [hereafter *WES*], July 29, 1954; "Final Rites Are Held for Mrs. Mary Church Terrell," *Atlanta Daily World* [hereafter *ADW*], August 4, 1954.

2. Quigley, *Just Another Southern Town*, 240; "Eisenhower Appoints Hayes Head of Capital Utilities Commission," *Chicago Defender* [hereafter *CD*], February 26, 1955.

3. Davis, "Black Power," 5, 13; Lincoln Temple United Church of Christ Archives.

4. Murphy, *Jim Crow Capital*, 5.

5. Asch and Musgrove, *Chocolate City*, 150–51; Melder, *City of Magnificent Intentions*, 473.

6. Quigley, *Just Another Southern Town*, 39.

7. Leslie, *History of the National Association of Colored Women's Clubs, Inc.*, unpaged.

8. Kelvin Muhia, "Objectives That Led to the National Association of Colored Women's Clubs," *Black Then: Discovering Our History*, July 21, 2018, www.Blackthen.com/objectives-led-national-association-colored-womens-club; "Convict Lease System," *WES*, July 18, 1901; "The Justice of Women's Suffrage," *Washington Times* [hereafter *WT*], February 10, 1900.

9. National Park Service, "The Niagara Movement at Harpers Ferry: Cornerstone of the Modern Civil Rights Era," https://www.nps.gov/hafe/learn/historyculture/the-niagara-movement.htm. Now defunct, the college's campus and buildings were acquired by the National Park Service as part of present-day Harpers Ferry Historical Park.
10. J. Milton Waldron to the Niagara Movement, February 26, 1909, credo.library.umass.edu/view/full/mums312-b004-i210; Fox, *Guardian of Boston*, 103.
11. Terrell, *Colored Woman in a White World*, 203–4.

1. "A Lively Response Was Manifested"

12. Asch and Musgrove, *Chocolate City*, 226.
13. Walker, "Struggles and Attempts to Establish Branch Autonomy," 22; "Leader in Many Good Movements," *BAA*, January 1, 1910; *Crisis* 4, no. 1 (May 1912), 23. No extant records document the precise date and venue that the D.C. branch of the NAACP informally organized. Primary sources suggest it was between March 1 and 14. A public interest meeting was held at Metropolitan AME Church on March 19, 1912, and the branch was formally established with a slate of elected officers on March 20, 1912.
14. Brooks-Higginbotham, *From Strength to Strength*, 99–104.
15. Ibid.
16. John Milton Waldron to Niagara Movement members, February 26, 1909, University of Massachusetts at Amherst, credo.library.umass.edu/view/full/mums312-b004-i210.
17. Moore, *Leading the Race*, 168–69.
18. Ibid.
19. Ibid.; "Help Alley Dwellers," *WES*, March 11, 1910; "Aid For Dwellers," *WES*, March 20, 1910; "Vacation Bible School Closes," *WES*, August 12, 1910.
20. "Will Hold Monster Meeting," *BAA*, March 16, 1912.
21. Ibid.
22. Mjagkij, *Organizing Black America*, 93–94.
23. *Crisis* 3, no. 6 (April 1912): 259.
24. Ibid.
25. *Crisis* 4, no. 1 (May 1912): 23; "Branch Is Formed Here," *WES*, April 13, 1912.

26. Slowe, "Notes," 480–82; *Crisis* (May 1912).

27. Kellogg, *NAACP*, 21–22.

28. Sullivan, *Lift Every Voice*, 22.

29. Ibid.

30. Ibid.; "Stafford, Wendell Phillips," Federal Judicial Center: https://www.fjc.gov/node/1388191; Asch and Musgrove, *Chocolate City*, 224.

31. "Will Hold Monster Meeting," *BAA*, March 16, 1912.

32. "Branch Is Formed Here," *WES*, April 13, 1912; "Capital Represented at Colored Enclave," *WT*, April 13, 1912.

33. "Welfare of the Colored People," *WES*, December 7, 1912.

34. Simmons, *Men of Mark*, 118.

35. "Another Movement," *Washington Bee* [hereafter *WB*], November 5, 1910.

36. Kellogg, *NAACP*, 23; "Another Movement," *WB*, November 5, 1910; DC Historic Preservation Office, "Civil Rights Tour: Civic Activism: Murray Brothers and the Black Press," *DC Historic Sites*, https://historicsites.dcpreservation.org/items/show/1057.

37. Lewis-Clark, *First Freed*, 64; Chase, "'Honey for Our Friends'"; Kellogg, *NAACP*, 54.

2. The Rise and Fall of the "Preacher-Politician"

38. Berg, *Wilson*, 269.

39. "Supporting Men and Measures Rather Than Parties," *Virginian-Piot and Norfolk Landmark*, August 31, 1912, National Association for the Advancement of Colored People Records, Library of Congress [hereafter NAACP Records].

40. "Wilson and Marshall Take Oath at Capitol While World Looks On," *WES*, March 4, 1913.

41. Berg, *Wilson*, 45–49, 132; Pestritto, *Woodrow Wilson*, 34; Mulder, *Woodrow Wilson*, 71–72.

42. Berg, *Wilson*, 155–58.

43. Ibid., 203.

44. Ibid., 189, 190, 236, 237.

45. Ibid., 237; Sullivan, *Lift Every Voice*, 26.

46. Berg, *Wilson*, 245; Schubert, "25th Infantry at Brownsville," 1,217–24.

47. Berg, *Wilson*, 245.

48. Ibid.

49. Ibid., 246.

50. Ibid., 246, 269.
51. *The Crisis* 4, no. 4 (August 1912), 181.
52. Ibid.
53. John Milton Waldron to Woodrow Wilson, October 21, 1910, WW Papers.
54. "Colored Men Revolt: Organize National League to Demand Fair Play," *Washington Post*, June 15, 1908.
55. Ibid.; "Taft Is Criticised: Negro Orators Denounce Republican Nominee," *WES*, August 10, 1908.
56. Waldron to Wilson, July 11, 1912, WW Papers.
57. "Supporting Men and Measures Rather Than Parties," *Virginian-Piot and Norfolk Landmark*, August 31, 1912, NAACP Records.
58. Ibid.
59. "Colored Pastors Honor Rev. J. Milton Waldron," *WT*, October 4, 1911.
60. Berg, *Wilson*, 247.
61. Asch and Musgrove, *Chocolate City*, 221.
62. Ibid.
63. Green, *Washington*, 216; Berg, *Wilson*, 307.
64. Berg, *Wilson*, 307.
65. Ibid., 262.
66. Ibid., 306.
67. Ibid., 220, 312.
68. Ibid., 251.
69. Thurber, "Negro at the Nation's Capital," 102–3.
70. "Southerners Best Friends: Colored Minister Addresses Meeting in Richmond, Va.," *Alexandria Gazette*, March 29, 1913.
71. Ibid.; Asch and Musgrove, *Chocolate City*, 224.
72. Goggin, *Carter G. Woodson*, 142; Perry, *Lift Up Thy Voice*, 335.
73. Walker, "Struggles and Attempts to Establish Branch Autonomy," 29–33; Asch and Musgrove, *Chocolate City*, 224.
74. "Officers Will Be Elected: Association for Advancement of Colored People to Meet," *WES*, April 18, 1913; Yellin, *Racism in the Nation's Service*, 106.
75. Yellin, *Racism in the Nation's Service*, 106.
76. Asch and Musgrove, *Chocolate City*, 224; Sullivan, *Lift Every Voice*, 29; *The Crisis* 6, no. 4 (August 1913), 190.
77. Mary White Ovington to May Childs Nerney, undated, NAACP Records.
78. Ibid.
79. "Washington Matter," June 22, 1913, NAACP Papers.
80. Ibid.

81. Ibid.; Waldron to NAACP Board of Directors, June 28, 1913, NAACP Papers; *Constitution of the District of Columbia Branch of the National Association for the Advancement of Colored People*, June 27, 1913, NAACP Papers.

82. Waldron to NAACP Board of Directors, June 28, 1913, NAACP Records.

83. Freeman H.M. Murray to W.E.B. Du Bois, June 28, 1913, NAACP Records.

84. Neval Thomas to Joel Spingarn, July 1913, Joel E. Spingarn Papers, Moorland-Spingarn Research Center, Howard University [hereafter JES Papers]; Walker, "Struggles and Attempts to Establish Branch Autonomy," 53–58.

85. Spingarn to Carrie Clifford, August 9, 1913, NAACP Papers.

86. Clifford to Spingarn, September 17, 1913, JES Papers.

3. New Battles and a "Red Summer"

87. Perry, *Lift Up Thy Voice*, 335.

88. Walker, "Struggles and Attempts to Establish Branch Autonomy," 46; Perry, *Lift Up Thy Voice*, 267–70.

89. Perry, *Lift Up Thy Voice*, 275, 288–90.

90. Ibid., 296–97.

91. Ibid.; Moore, *Leading the Race*, 195–97.

92. Perry, *Lift Up Thy Voice*, 299.

93. Moses Clapp and Oswald Villard Correspondence, September 12–16, 1913, NAACP Papers.

94. Sullivan, *Lift Every Voice*, 30; NAACP to Wilson, August 15, 1913, WW Papers.

95. Archibald Grimke Papers, September 1913, Moorland-Spingarn Research Center, Howard University [hereafter AG Papers].

96. Ibid.; Berg, *Wilson*, 309; Sullivan, *Lift Every Voice*, 29; Feagin, *Systemic Racism*, 162.

97. Sullivan, *Lift Every Voice*, 29; Thurber, "Negro at the Nation's Capital," 57–58; DC-NAACP Letter and Resolution Against Segregation to Wilson from Grimké, October 29, 1913, WW Papers.

98. Sullivan, *Lift Every Voice*, 30–31.

99. Thurber, "Negro at the Nation's Capital," 50, 70; *The Crisis* 7, no. 4 (February 1914): 192–94.

100. Thurber, "Negro at the Nation's Capital," 109–11.

101. Ibid.

102. Sullivan, *Lift Every Voice*, 31; Thurber, "Negro at the Nation's Capital," 118.

103. Lehr, *Birth of a Nation*, 150.

104. Ibid., 151–55.

105. Ibid., 150.

106. W.A. Adams to W.E.B. Du Bois, February 9, 1916, NAACP Records.

107. AG Papers, September-October 1915; Berg, *Wilson*, 349–50.

108. "NAACP Not a 'Black Hand,'" *BAA*, March 4, 1916.

109. Ibid.

110. "The Star of Ethiopia Pleases," *BAA*, October 16, 1915.

111. Ibid.; "'Rachel,' A Race Play Given by Local Cast," *WES*, March 4, 1916.

112. Thurber, "Negro at the Nation's Capital," 127–28; "A Bill to Prohibit Exhibition or Use of Films or Pictorial Representations Calculated to Reflect on Any Race or Nationality," AG Papers, April 15, 1916.

113. "At the Washington Theaters: National—Birth of a Nation," *WES*, April 17, 1916.

114. Letter to Grimké from "Mr. Portlock," May 1916, AG Papers; Sullivan, *Lift Every Voice*, 31; Thurber, "Negro at the Nation's Capital," 129.

115. "Action Against Production of 'The Birth of a Nation,'" undated, NAACP Records.

116. "Fight Upon Film May Go to Court," *WES*, April 12, 1916.

117. Grimké to Moorfield Storey, 1918, NAACP Records; "An Unpopular Selection," *BAA*, June 27, 1919.

118. Carl Mapes and Frederick Gillette to Grimké, July 16, 1919, Grimke Papers; Haskins, *Evening Star*, 46; DC Branch of NAACP to general membership, July 23, 1919, NAACP Records.

119. Krugler, *1919*, 72–73.

120. Ibid., 75–77; Asch and Musgrove, *Chocolate City*, 233.

121. Krugler, *1919*, 223.

122. Ibid., 78–79, 223; Asch and Musgrove, *Chocolate City*, 233.

123. Krugler, *1919*, 88, 90, 94; St. Louis, Missouri and Providence, Rhode Island NAACP branch correspondence to Grimké, July 1919, AG Papers.

124. Kluger, *Simple Justice*, 224–28.

125. Correspondence to Grimké from Fred Morton and Thomas Redd, October 1919, AG Papers.

126. Goggin, *Carter G. Woodson*, 141–48.

127. Kluger, *Simple Justice*, 94–97.

128. Ibid., 96.

4. *"Don't Let the Ku Klux Catch You Napping!"*

129. Neval Thomas to Walter McCoy, November 1919; Thomas and Mary White Ovington correspondence, November–December 1919, NAACP Records.

130. Walker, "Struggles and Attempts to Establish Branch Autonomy," 138–40.

131. "What Has the Branch Done: A Record of the Efforts and Achievements of the District of Columbia Branch of the National Association for the Advancement of Colored People During the Year 1919," April 1920, NAACP Records.

132. Quigley, *Just Another Southern Town*, 98; "Report of the District of Columbia Branch of the National Association for the Advancement of Colored People to the Twelfth Annual Conference at Detroit, Michigan, June 26–July 1, 1921," NAACP Records.

133. Shelby Davidson to James Weldon Johnson, March 22, 1922, NAACP Records.

134. "Klan Has Many Members Here." *WES*, September 25, 1921.

135. "Parade in Cumberland" and "Masked Men in Church," *BAA*, March 24, 1922.

136. "Check Klan Parades," *CD*, April 1, 1922.

137. Sullivan, *Lift Every Voice*, 75; *Supplement to The Crisis* 12, no. 3 (July 1916): 1–8.

138. Armstrong, "'People…Took Exception to Her Remarks,'" 113–41.

139. Brown, *Eradicating This Evil*, 110–11.

140. Ibid., 138; Zangrando and Lewis, *Walter F. White*, 34.

141. Quigley, *Just Another Southern Town*, 102–9.

142. Ibid.

143. Shelby Davidson to James Weldon Johnson, March 7, 1922, NAACP Records; "100,000 Hear Dr. R.R. Moton Laud Lincoln," *CD*, June 2, 1922; Quigley, *Just Another Southern Town*, 102–9; "Resolution of Protest Adopted by the District of Columbia Branch of the NAACP Against the Segregation of Colored People at the Lincoln Memorial," June 7, 1922, NAACP Records.

144. Thomas, "These 'Colored' United States," 837–41.

145. Murphy, *Jim Crow Capital*, 52.

146. NAACP-District of Columbia Branch Records, Box 78–63, Folders 1391–1394, Moorland-Spingarn Research Center, Howard University [hereafter NAACP-DC Records].

147. "Silent Protest Parade Against Lynching, Celebrates the Birth of Old Glory," June 1922, NAACP Records; Murphy, *Jim Crow Capital*, 53–55.

148. McElya, *Clinging to Mammy*, 140–47.

149. Ibid.

150. "Old Mammies Memorial," *WES*, January 31, 1923.

151. "Southerners Put More Value on Human Slavery Than on Virtue, Seek Location in D.C.," *Washington Tribune*, February 23, 1923.

152. "Sees Mark of Servitude: Correspondent Disapproves Move For 'Old Mammies' Memorial," *WES*, February 6, 1923.

153. Shelby Davidson to James Weldon Johnson, February 3, 1923, NAACP Records.

154. James Weldon Johnson to Shelby Davidson, February 5, 1923, NAACP Records.

155. "The Black Mammy Monument," *WES*, February 10, 1923.

156. McElya, *Clinging to Mammy*, 140–47; "Model of Mammy Statue Made By Ex-DC Student," *WES*, March 22, 1923; "Rival's 'Mammy' Statue Arouses Artist's Wrath, *WP*, June 28, 1923.

157. "Voice Protest Against Mammy Statue," *Washington Tribune*, February 10, 1923; "DC Newspaper Suggests Bomb for Proposed Monument to 'Black Mammies,'" *BAA*, March 9, 1923.

158. "Answers to Questions," *WES*, July 30, 1923.

159. James Cobb to Arthur Spingarn, January 5, 1924, AG Papers.

160. Arthur Spingarn to James Cobb, January 8, 1924, AG Papers; "Value of Public Library," *Washington Herald*, October 12, 1922.

161. "Student Training Class: The Public Library of the District of Columbia," 1922, DC Public Library Archives, The People's Archive, DC Public Library.

162. "The Library and Colored People," *WH*, October 15, 1922.

163. "Makes Personal Visit to Librarian," *Washington Eagle*, November 4, 1922; "Twentieth Annual Report of the Board of Trustees and Nineteenth Annual Report of the Librarian of the Public Library of the District of Columbia" (Washington, 1917), Collection 40: DCPL Archives, TPA, DCPL.

164. "Washington NAACP Scores Library Jim Crow System," *BAA*, February 28, 1925.

165. "African Americans and the Library," Index to DCPL Board of Trustees Minutes, TPA, DCPL.

166. Daniel Garges to Kelly Miller, May 29, 1925; Kelly Miller to James Weldon Johnson, June 25, 1925, NAACP Records.

167. Ibid.

168. "District Grants Klan Permit To Parade 200,000 Men in City," *WES*, June 17, 1925.

169. "N.B. After July 4, 1925," Collection 147, Lucy G. Barber Collection, The People's Archive, DCPL.

170. "Klan's 1925 Rally: A 'Great Parade,'" *WP*, November 29, 1982.

171. Ibid.; "18,000 Night Shirts in DC Klan Parade," *BAA*, September 18, 1926.

172. Hyatt, "Neval H. Thomas," 96–97, 100–102.

173. "Kelly Miller Says," *BAA*, December 27, 1924.

174. Hyatt, "Neval H. Thomas," 101; "Quits Colored Post," *WES*, January 19, 1928.

175. "Neval Thomas, Militant NAACP Leader, Mourned," *BAA*, April 19, 1930.

5. *"Make Pennsylvania Avenue Tremble!"*

176. Ibid.

177. Ibid.; "NAACP to Honor Grimke and Thomas," *BAA*, October 19, 1930.

178. "Neval Thomas's $500 to Work of NAACP," *BAA*, September 19, 1931; "Miss Merritt Chosen Head of Association," *WES*, May 29, 1930; Taylor, "Emma Frances Grayson Merritt," 3–4.

179. Taylor, "Emma Frances Grayson Merritt," 3–4; "Minutes of the Board of Education of the District of Columbia, Volume 20, July 1, 1929–June 25, 1930," Charles Sumner School Museum and Archives.

180. "NAACP Watching D.C. Police Dept.," *BAA*, August 30, 1930.

181. "Police Third Degree Brutality Described at NAACP Meet," *BAA*, June 21, 1930.

182. "Virginia G. McGuire, Leader in Battle for Civil Rights Here," *WP*, February 4, 1967.

183. Murphy, *Jim Crow Capital*, 87.

184. Ibid., 88.

185. Ibid.

186. Ibid., 62, 91.

187. Ibid., 64; Zangrando and Lewis, *Walter F. White*, 106–7; "Legal Defense: Discussion at the Twenty-third Annual Conference of the National Association for the Advancement of Colored People, Washington, DC, May 20, 1932," NAACP Records.

188. Murphy, *Jim Crow Capital*, 64; "Mrs. Roosevelt Urges Equality," *WES*, April 15, 1935.

189. Virginia McGuire to Nannie Helen Burroughs, March 27, 1934, NAACP Records.

190. Ibid.

191. Ibid., 65; "Jail Anti-Lynch Pickets at Crime Confab!," *ADW*, December 12, 1934.

192. Ibid., 65–68.

193. Ibid.

194. "Don't Be Cowards Nannie Burroughs Tells Washington," *BAA*, January 5, 1935.

195. "Bruce Heads DC Branch of NAACP," *BAA*, November 1935.

196. Pacifico, "'Don't Buy Where You Can't Work,'" 66–88.

197. Ibid.; "Hecht's to Keep J.C. Restrooms," *BAA*, May 23, 1936.

198. "Election Rift Divides Unit," *BAA*, January 23, 1937.

199. Nannie Helen Burroughs to Walter White, January 29, 1937, NAACP Records.

200. "Incorporated NAACP Branch Loses Charter," *BAA*, May 15, 1937.

201. "NAACP Is Victor in Fight," *ADW*, January 21, 1939.

202. "New DC Branch of NAACP," *CD*, March 18, 1939; "NAACP Seeks 5,000 Members in Drive," *BAA*, March 18, 1939; "Dr. Marshall to Head Revamped NAACP Unit," *BAA*, May 13, 1939.

203. Craig Simpson, "Shootings by DC Police Spark Fight Against Brutality 1936–1941," *Washington Area Spark*, April 20, 2013, https://washingtonareaspark.com/2013/04/20/shootings-by-dc-police-spark-fight-against-brutality-1936-41/.

204. C. Herbert Marshall to Walter White, April 15, 1939, NAACP-District of Columbia Branch Records.

205. "Co-operation That Counts," *WT*, December 16, 1939.

206. "Colored Pastor Here 22 Years Succumbs," *WES*, November 20, 1931; "Mrs. Clifford, One of NAACP Founders, Dies," *BAA*, November 17, 1934.

6. On the National Stage

207. Kluger, *Simple Justice*, 513–14.

208. Ibid.

209. McQuirter, "'Our Cause Is Marching On,'" 66–82.

210. Ibid.

211. Ibid.; Kluger, *Simple Justice*, 515.

212. McQuirter, "'Our Cause Is Marching On,'" 66–82; Asch and Musgrove, *Chocolate City*, 307.

213. McQuirter, "'Our Cause Is Marching On,'" 66–82.

214. Ibid.

215. Kluger, *Simple Justice*, 517.

216. McQuirter, "'Our Cause Is Marching On,'" 66–82; "'Separate But Equal' Schools Theory Ruling by DC Court to Be Appealed," *BAA*, February 25, 1950.

217. Kluger, *Simple Justice*, 519.

218. Ibid., 522–23.

219. Asch and Musgrove, *Chocolate City*, 312.

220. "Propose $5,000,000 For More Jim Crow Schools In Capital," *CD*, June 7, 1952; "DC Desegregation Activist Gardner L. Bishop Dies at Age 82," *WP*, November 27, 1992.

221. Asch and Musgrove, *Chocolate City*, 312.

222. Quigley, *Just Another Southern Town*, 145, 228.

223. Ibid.

224. Asch and Musgrove, *Chocolate City*, 313.

225. Burk, *Eisenhower Administration and Black Civil Rights*, 56; "'Gradual' Integration Plan Scored By NAACP," *WP*, May 31, 1954.

226. "Capital Spotlight," *BAA*, December 1, 1951.

227. "'Gradual' Integration Plan Scored by NAACP," *WP*, May 31, 1954; Eugene Davidson, "The State of the Nation's Capital: An Excerpt From the Annual Report, D.C. Branch, National Association for the Advancement of Colored People," December 18, 1955, Washingtoniana Vertical Files Collection, The People's Archive, DC Public Library.

228. Telegram to Nannie Helen Burroughs, March 27, 1957, Nannie Helen Burroughs Papers, Library of Congress [hereafter as NHB Papers].

229. "King on Stage at Howard University: 1956," Flickr, https://flickr.com/photos/washington_area_spark/34965912114; "4,000 D.C. Citizens Hear Rev. M.L. King," *BAA*, December 15, 1956.

230. Gray, "Remaining Awake Through a Great Revolution," 10–19.

231. Ibid.

232. "Pilgrimage Post-Mortem: Many Present But Some 'Play Hooky,'" *BAA*, June 1, 1957.

233. "Pilgrim Sees 'Dead Town' Rise with Welcome Mat," *BAA*, May 25, 1957.

234. "Pilgrimage Post-Mortem: Many Present but Some 'Play Hooky,'" *BAA*, June 1, 1957; "So…This Is Washington," *CD*, June 29, 1957.

235. A. Philp Randolph Papers, Box 31, Library of Congress [hereafter APR Papers].

236. Prayer Pilgrimage Program, undated, APR Papers; "In the Fight to Stay," *BAA*, July 28, 1917; Nannie Helen Burroughs to Martin Luther King Jr., NHB Papers.

237. "Pilgrimage Post-Mortem."

238. "Breaking of Woman's Arm Described as a Heinous Act," *BAA*, July 4, 1953.

239. "NAACP Presses Discipline Issue," *BAA*, May 26, 1956; Julius Hobson Papers, The People's Archive, DC Public Library.

240. "District NAACP Head Calls for Murray Ouster," *WES*, June 7, 1957.

241. "Murray Requests Speedy Hearing," *WP*, July 3, 1957; "City Heads Back Murray in Bias Claim," *WP*, July 4, 1957.

242. "NAACP Claims Harassment, Insults in Detailing Police Brutality Changes," *WP*, July 13, 1957.

243. "NAACP Asks Whole FBI Police Probe," *BAA*, July 27, 1957.

244. "Murray Takes Stand in Bias Case Today," *WP*, October 30, 1957.

245. "Police Bias Is Denied by Murray," *WP*, November 1, 1957; Marie Maxwell, "NAACP vs. the Washington DC Police Department: A 1957 Hearing Before the DC Board of Commissioners," *National Archives: The Text Message*, November 28, 2014, https://text-message.blogs.archives.gov/2014/11/28/naacp-vs-the-washington-dc-police-department-a-1957-hearing-before-the-dc-board-of-commissioners.

246. "Chief Murray Is Exonerated of Police Bias," *WP*, November 8, 1957.

247. "Gains In Rights, Job Opportunities in D.C.," *ADW*, January 2, 1959.

248. Borchardt, "Making D.C. Democracy's Capital," 130.

249. Reddick, *Crusader Without Violence*, 265.

250. "NAACP Washington Report Finds Housing Picture Dark," *BAA*, December 28, 1957; "On NAACP Battlefront: 60,000 Members Proposed for DC," *BAA*, February 7, 1959.

7. Jousting Philosophies and the Triumph of Black Power

251. Borchardt, "Making D.C. Democracy's Capital," 132.

252. Julius Hobson to Gloster Current, October 17, 1960, NAACP Records.

253. Borchardt, "Making D.C. Democracy's Capital," 131.

254. Ibid., 132.

255. Ibid., 133.

256. Ibid., 134–35.

257. Ibid., 137.

258. "'Leave Us Alone,' CORE Tells NAACP," *WAA*, January 27, 1962.

259. "Picket Line of F Street Protests 'Growing Tide' of Discrimination," *WP*, February 25, 1962.

260. "The Listless D.C. NAACP: Politics, Fear or Lethargy?" *WAA*, September 29, 1962.

261. Ibid.

262. Dolph Thompson to Roy Wilkins, February 19, 1963, NAACP Records.

263. Gloster Current to Dolph Thompson, March 11, 1963, NAACP Records.

264. "NAACP Head, Layton Clash on Police Methods," *WP*, March 14, 1963.

265. Ibid.

266. "Rev. Hailes of New Bedford New DC NAACP Exec. Sec.," *BAA*, February 9, 1963.

267. Asch and Musgrove, *Chocolate City*, 338.

268. Burns, *To the Mountaintop*, 210.

269. "Meredith Doubts Value of DC March, Hits Young Negro Leaders; Is Rebuked," *WES*, July 6, 1963.

270. "In Our Churches: Dr. Jackson Booed., *New York Amsterdam News*, July 13, 1963; "A Mass Demonstration?" *WES*, July 6, 1963.

271. Ibid.

272. "Now About That March…" *WAA*, July 13, 1963.

273. Gray and Krafchik, "'Its Fingers Were Crossed,'" 20–35.

274. Ibid.

275. "Evers' Widow Urges Rally to Take Up Cause," *WES*, August 26, 1963.

276. Gray and Krafchik, "'Its Fingers Were Crossed,'" 20–35; George Lincoln Rockwell to Governor Albertis Harrison, Virginia Governor (1962–1966: Harrison), Executive Papers, 1962–1966, Accession 26231 and 26833, State government records collection, the Library of Virginia, Richmond, Virginia; "Rockwell Nazis 'Kaput' in Counter Move: Aimed at 10,000 Speaker Permit Denied," *WP*, August 29, 1963.

277. "Malcolm X at Uline Arena," Black Power in Washington, D.C., 1961–1998, https://experience.arcgis.com/experience/5e17e7d1c4a840 6b9eaf26a4eae77103/page/Origins%2C-1961-65-Map/; "'Whites Made Washington March a Farce,' Declares Malcolm X," *CD*, October 10, 1963.

278. March on Washington 50th Anniversary Oral History Project, The People's Archive, DC Public Library [digdc.dclibrary.org/islandora/object/dcplislandora%3A42427].

279. "NAACP Head Quits To Seek Party Post," *WP*, January 10, 1964.

280. Asch and Musgrove, *Chocolate City*, 339.

281. "'Rat Rally' Nets 100 Spectators but No Rats," *WP*, August 23, 1964.

282. Pearlman, *Democracy's Capital*, 55; Smith, *Captive Capital*, 237; "Inside a Citizens Council Meeting in a U.S. Armory," *BAA*, October 3, 1964.

283. Pearlman, *Democracy's Capital*, 31–32.

284. Rohal, "Teachable Moment," 49–52.

285. Ibid.

286. Ibid.

287. Ibid., 34–38.

288. "King's Dream: Vote Is Key to Solution of City's Problems," *WP*, August 9, 1965; "Capital Takes Dr. King to Its Heart," *BAA*, August 14, 1965.

289. Pearlman, *Democracy's Capital*, 38.

290. Ibid., 35.

291. Ibid., 37; "NAACP Drops Support of Free D.C. Campaign," *WP*, March 12, 1966; "NAACP Balks at Boycott in DC," *CD*, March 31, 1966.

292. "NAACP's Free D.C. Policy Puzzling," *WP*, April 6, 1966.

293. Pearlman, *Democracy's Capital*, 37–38.

294. Davis, "Black Power," 5, 13; Lincoln Temple United Church of Christ Archives.

295. "Negroes Optimistic but Remain Militant," *WP*, October 6, 1966.

296. Ibid.

297. Ibid.; Asch and Musgrove, *Chocolate City*, 352.

298. "KKK Note Is Posted at NAACP," *BAA*, October 15, 1966.

299. "Leaderless and Broke, City's NAACP Branch Is Marking Time," *WP*, November 3, 1967.

300. Ibid.; Pearlman, *Democracy's Capital*, 61.

301. "NAACP in Appeal For Law, Order," *BAA*, September 17, 1966; Pearlman, *Democracy's Capital*, 60–61.

302. "Lawyer, 28, Takes Post in NAACP," *WES*, November 21, 1967; "Fund-Short NAACP Branch Here Fills Long Vacant Director's Post," *WP*, November 22, 1967.

303. "Digital SNCC Gateway: Nonviolent Action Group (NAG)," snccdigital. org/inside-sncc/establishing-sncc/campus-affiliates/nonviolent-action-group-nag/; Asch and Musgrove, *Chocolate City*, 342–43.

304. Asch and Musgrove, *Chocolate City*, 353–54; "Mayor, Stokely Talk Likely," *WES*, January 15, 1968.

305. "Carmichael Holds Secret Impact," *CD*, January 15, 1968; Chuck Stone oral history interview, April 11, 1999, *OHP #020: DC Statehood Movement Leaders*, TPA, DCPL; Pearlman, *Democracy's Capital*, 54.

306. Pearlman, *Democracy's Capital*, 55; "Black United Front Hits Snag," *CD*, January 27, 1968.

307. Pearlman, *Democracy's Capital*, 55.

308. Barber, *Marching on Washington*, 177.

309. Washington Spark, https://washingtonareaspark.com; Gray, "Remaining Awake Through a Great Revolution," 10–19.

310. Gray, "Remaining Awake Through a Great Revolution," 10–19.

311. "King Acts to Mend Disagreement in Civil Rights Ranks," *WP*, October 15, 1966; "Wilkins Sees Violence During DC March," *CD*, April 4, 1968.

312. "King Issue Widens NAACP Rift," *WP*, March 20, 1968; "Local NAACP Backs King's Jobs Drive," *WES*, March 18, 1968.

313. South of U Oral History Project—Life, Riots, and Renewal in Shaw, The People's Archive, DC Public Library, https://digdc.dclibrary.org/; Gilbert, *Ten Blocks from the White House*, 21.

314. Pearlman, *Democracy's Capital*, 66.

315. Ibid., 69–70.

316. Ibid., 72.

317. "Mayor, Stokely Talk Likely," *WES*, January 10, 1968; "DC Leaders Show Grief, Ire," *WES*, April 5, 1968; "Emergency Food Is Available for Victims of DC Violence," *WES*, April 7, 1968; "Looting, Arson Continue, Some Easing Is Reported," *WES*, April 7, 1968; Gilbert, *Ten Blocks from the White House*, 213.

318. "DC Estimates 2500 Lost Jobs From Rioting," *WP*, April 10, 1968.

319. Ibid., "Emergency Food Is Available for Victims of DC Violence," *WES*, April 7, 1968; "NAACP Here Plagued By Lack of Funds, Help," *WP*, August 13, 1968.

320. "DC Leaders Show Grief, Ire," *WES*, April 5, 1968; "So This Is Washington," *CD*, April 27, 1968.

321. "NAACP Is Puzzled by Membership Drop," *WP*, September 16, 1968; Pearlman, "More Than a March," 24–39.

322. "NAACP Plagued Here by Lack of Funds, Help," *WP*, August 13, 1968.

323. "Local NAACP Officer Slate Is Nominated," *WP*, November 19, 1968; "District NAACP Unit Elects Hailes President," *WES*, December 8, 1968.

324. Asch and Musgrove, *Chocolate City*, 378–81.

BIBLIOGRAPHY

Archival Sources

Albertis S. Harrison Executive Papers, Library of Virginia

A. Philip Randolph Papers, Library of Congress

Archibald Grimke Papers, Moorland-Spingarn Research Center, Howard University

DC-NAACP Branch Records, Moorland-Spingarn Research Center, Howard University

DC Statehood Movement Leaders Oral History Project, The People's Archive, DC Public Library

District of Columbia Public Library Records, The People's Archive, DC Public Library

Eugene Davidson Papers, Moorland-Spingarn Research Center, Howard University

Joel Spingarn Papers, Moorland-Spingarn Research Center, Howard University

Julius Hobson Papers, The People's Archive, DC Public Library

Lucy Barber Collection, The People's Archive, DC Public Library

March on Washington 50th Anniversary Oral History Project, The People's Archive, DC Public Library

Minutes of the Board of Education of the District of Columbia, Charles Sumner School Museum and Archives

Nannie Helen Burroughs Papers, Library of Congress

National Association for the Advancement of Colored People Records, Library of Congress

South of U Oral History Project, The People's Archive, DC Public Library

Washingtoniana Vertical Files Collection, The People's Archive, DC Public Library

Woodrow Wilson Papers, Library of Congress

Newspapers

Alexandria (VA) Gazette
Atlanta Daily World
Baltimore Afro-American
Chicago Defender
New York Amsterdam News
Washington Afro-American
Washington Eagle
Washington Evening Star
Washington Post
Washington Times
Washington Tribune

Articles

Armstrong, Julie Buckner. "'The People…Took Exception to Her Remarks': Meta Warrick Fuller, Angelina Grimke and the Lynching of Mary Turner." *Mississippi Quarterly*, Winter–Spring 2008.

Davis, Minnie. "Black Power: Good or Bad?" *The Lincoln Reporter*, September–October 1966.

Gray, Derek. "'Remaining Awake Through a Great Revolution': Martin Luther King, Jr.'s Legacy of Activism in Washington, D.C." *Washington History* 30 (Fall 2018): 10–19.

Gray, Derek, and Jennifer Krafchik. "'Its Fingers Were Crossed and Its Guard Was Up': Washington Prepares for the March for Jobs and Freedom." *Washington History* 25 (Summer 2013): 20–35.

Hyatt, Marshall. "Neval H. Thomas and Federal Segregation." *Negro History Bulletin* 42, no. 4 (October–December 1979): 96–102.

McQuirter, Marya. "'Our Cause Is Marching On': Parent Activism, Browne Junior High School and the Meanings of Equality in Post-War Washington." *Washington History* 16, no. 2 (Fall 2004/Winter 2005): 66–82.

Pacifico, Michele F. "'Don't Buy Where You Can't Work': The New Negro Alliance in Washington." *Washington History* 6, no. 1 (Spring/Summer 1994): 66–88.

Pearlman, Lauren. "More Than a March: The Poor People's Campaign in the District." *Washington History* 26, no. 2 (Fall 2014): 24–41.

Rohal, Brian. "Teachable Moment: Mobilizing the Community in an Era Before Social Media." *Washington History* 28 (Spring 2016): 49–52.

Schubert, Frank N. "The 25th Infantry at Brownsville, Texas: Buffalo Soldiers, 'The Brownsville Six' and the Medal of Honor." *Journal of Military History* 75, no. 4 (October 2011): 1217–24.

Slowe, Lucy D. "Notes." *Journal of Negro History* 16, no. 4 (October 1931): 480–82.

Taylor, Estelle W. "Emma Frances Grayson Merritt: Pioneer in Negro Education." *Negro History Bulletin* 38, no. 6 (January–September 1996): 434.

Thomas, Neval H. "These 'Colored' United States: The District of Columbia—A Paradise of Paradoxes." *The Messenger* 5, no. 10 (October 1923): 837–41.

Secondary Sources

Asch, Chris Myers, and George Derek Musgrove. *Chocolate City: A History of Race and Democracy in the Nation's Capital.* Chapel Hill: University of North Carolina Press, 2017.

Barber, Lucy G. *Marching on Washington: The Forging of an American Political Tradition.* Berkeley: University of California Press, 2002.

Berg, A. Scott. *Wilson.* New York: Penguin, 2013.

Borchardt, Gregory M. "Making D.C. Democracy's Capital: Local Activism, the 'Federal State,' and the Struggle for Civil Rights in D.C." Ph.D. diss., George Washington University, 2013.

Brooks-Higginbotham, Evelyn. *From Strength to Strength: The History of the Shiloh Baptist Church of Washington, DC, 1863–1988.* Washington, D.C.: Shiloh Baptist Church, 1988.

Brown, Mary Jane. *Eradicating This Evil: Women in the American Anti-Lynching Movement, 1892–1940.* New York: Garland Publishing, 2000.

Burk, Robert Fredrick. *The Eisenhower Administration and Black Civil Rights*. Knoxville: University of Tennessee/Knoxville Press, 1984.

Burns, Stewart. *To the Mountaintop: Martin Luther King, Jr.'s Sacred Mission to Save America*. New York: HarperCollins Publishers, 2004.

Chase, Hal Scripps. "'Honey For Our Friends, Stings for Enemies': William Calvin Chase and the Washington Bee, 1882–1921." PhD diss., University of Pennsylvania, 1973.

Feagin, Joe R. *Systemic Racism: A Theory of Oppression*. New York: Taylor & Francis, 2006.

Fox, Stephen R. *The Guardian of Boston: William Monroe Trotter*. New York: Antheum Press, 1970.

Gilbert, Ben W. *Ten Blocks from the White House: Anatomy of the Washington Riots of 1968*. New York: Frederick A. Praeger, 1968.

Goggin, Jacqueline. *Carter G. Woodson: A Life in Black History*. Baton Rouge: Louisiana State University Press, 1993.

Green, Constance McLaughlin. *Washington: A History of the Capital, 1800–1950*. Princeton, NJ: Princeton University Press, 1962.

Haskins, Faye. *The Evening Star: The Rise and Fall of a Great Washington Newspaper*. Lanham, MD: Roman & Littlefield, 2019.

Kellogg, Charles Flint. *NAACP: A History of the National Association for the Advancement of Colored People*. Vol. 1, *1909–1920*. Baltimore, MD: Johns Hopkins Press, 1973.

Kluger, Richard. *Simple Justice: The History of Brown v. Board of Education and Black America's Struggle for Equality*. New York: Alfred A. Knopf, 2004.

Krugler, David F. *1919, The Year of Racial Violence: How African Americans Fought Back*. New York: Cambridge University Press, 2015.

Lehr, Dick. *The Birth of a Nation: How a Legendary Filmmaker and a Crusading Editor Reignited America's Civil War*. New York: Public Affairs, 2014.

Leslie, LaVonne. *The History of the National Association of Colored Women's Clubs, Inc.: A Legacy of Service*. Bloomington, IN: Xlibris Corporation, 2012.

Lewis-Clark, Elizabeth. *First Freed: Washington, D.C. in the Emancipation Era*. Washington, D.C.: Howard University Press, 2002.

McElya, Micki. *Clinging to Mammy: The Faithful Slave in Twentieth Century America*. Cambridge, MA: Harvard University Press, 2007.

Melder, Keith. *City of Magnificent Intentions: A History of the District of Columbia*. Washington, D.C.: Intac Inc., 1983.

Mjagkij, Nina. *Organizing Black America: An Encyclopedia of African American Associations*. New York: Garland Publishing, Inc., 2001.

Moore, Jacqueline M. *Leading the Race: The Transformation of the Black Elite in the Nation's Capital, 1880–1920.* Charlottesville: University of Virginia Press, 1999.

Mulder, John H. *Woodrow Wilson: The Years of Preparation.* Princeton, NJ: Princeton University Press, 1978.

Murphy, Mary Elizabeth B. *Jim Crow Capital: Women and Black Freedom Struggles in Washington, D.C., 1920–1945.* Chapel Hill: University of North Carolina Press, 2018.

Pearlman, Lauren. *Democracy's Capital: Black Political Power In Washington, D.C., 1960s–1970s.* Chapel Hill: University of North Carolina Press, 2019.

Perry, Mark. *Lift Up Thy Voice: The Sarah and Angelina Grimke Family's Journey from Slaveholders to Civil Rights Leaders.* London: Penguin Books, 2001.

Pestritto, Ronald J. *Woodrow Wilson and the Roots of Modern Liberalism.* Lanham, MD: Rowman and Littlefield, 2005.

Quigley, Joan. *Just Another Southern Town: Mary Church Terrell and the Struggle for Racial Justice in the Nation's Capital.* New York: Oxford University Press, 2016.

Reddick, L.D. *Crusader Without Violence: A Biography of Martin Luther King, Jr.* Montgomery, AL: NewSouth Books, 2018.

Simmons, William J. *Men of Mark: Eminent, Progressive, and Rising.* Cleveland, OH: George Rewell and Company, 1887.

Smith, Sam. *Captive Capital: Colonial Life in Modern Washington.* Bloomington: Indiana University Press, 1974.

Sullivan, Patricia. *Lift Every Voice: The NAACP and the Making of the Civil Rights Movement.* New York: New Press, 2009.

Terrell, Mary Church. *A Colored Woman in a White World.* Amherst, NY: Humanity Books, 2005.

Thurber, Bert H. "The Negro at the Nation's Capital, 1913-1921." PhD diss., Yale University, 1973.

Walker, Lewis Newton, Jr. "The Struggles and Attempts to Establish Branch Autonomy and Hegemony: A History of the District of Columbia Branch, National Association For the Advancement of Colored People, 1912–1942." Ph.D. diss., University of Delaware, 1979.

Yellin, Eric S. *Racism in the Nation's Service: Government Workers and the Color Line in Woodrow Wilson's America.* Chapel Hill: University of North Carolina Press, 2013.

Zangrando, Robert L., and Ronald L. Lewis. *Walter F. White: The NAACP's Ambassador for Racial Justice.* Morgantown: West Virginia University Press, 2019.

INDEX

W

Waldron, John Milton 18, 24, 29,
 31, 33, 35, 36, 37, 38, 40, 41,
 47, 48, 49, 50, 54, 55, 56, 57,
 58, 59, 60, 61, 64, 65, 76, 79,
 82, 83, 109, 123, 127, 159,
 194, 196, 197
Washington Afro-American 17, 38, 71,
 76, 87, 107, 108, 123, 138,
 141, 151, 158, 159, 180
Washington Bee 39, 40, 54, 62
Washington, Booker T. 20, 23, 44,
 54, 62, 68
Washington Eagle 85, 101, 102
Washington Evening Star 17, 19, 38,
 41, 71, 72, 77, 87, 97, 98, 100,
 101, 107, 146, 150, 164, 173
Washington, Jesse 88, 90, 96
Washington Post 38, 73, 78, 79, 81,
 100, 107, 150, 174, 176, 177,
 186
Washington Tribune 98, 123, 127
Washington, Walter 183
White, Walter 120
Wilkins, Roy 117, 120, 139, 144,
 153, 156, 159, 163, 180, 182
Williams, Dudley 179, 186, 187
Wilson, Woodrow 26, 41, 42, 43,
 44, 45, 46, 47, 48, 49, 50, 51,
 52, 53, 55, 56, 60, 65, 66, 69,
 71, 76, 81, 85, 86, 87, 107
Woodson, Carter G. 35, 78, 82, 83,
 102, 111, 115, 151

Z

Zolnay, George Julian 100

ABOUT THE AUTHOR

*D*erek Gray is an archivist in The People's Archive at the DC Public Library. He has a passion for the preservation, documentation and presentation of the African American experience in Washington. He has contributed several articles for *Washington History*, the scholarly journal of the DC History Center and is one of four coauthors of *Angels of Deliverance: The Underground Railroad in Queens, Long Island, and Beyond* (Queens Historical Society, 1999).